PU

THE
INVESTIGATO...

'I do not feel the smallest ...
and I am pretty confident ... world
will have accepted this before AD 2000.'
– *Frederick Myers, psychic researcher, in 1890*

[Enter, a Ghost]
– *William Shakespeare (stage-direction); Hamlet*

'I think we can be pretty sure that there are some genuine
mysteries out there. But right now, we have no answers,
only questions.'
– *John Spencer, ghost hunter*

'I can promise nothing of ghosts – when people wish to
hear them, they do not, I have found.'
– *Bob Parsons, owner of a haunted house*

'From ghoulies and ghosties and long-legged beasties and
things that go bump in the night, good Lord deliver us.'
– *Old Scottish prayer*

'I ain't afraid of no ghosts!'
– *The* Ghostbusters *theme tune*

'The Poltergeist is mischievous, destructive, noisy, cruel,
erratic, thievish ...'
– *Harry Price, ghost hunter*

'And I'd have gotten away with it too – if it hadna been for
you meddling kids!'
– *The baddie at the end of every single episode of* Scooby
Doo *ever*

The Ghost Investigator's Handbook

Marc Gascoigne

PUFFIN BOOKS

PUFFIN BOOKS

Published by the Penguin Group
Penguin Books Ltd, 27 Wrights Lane, London W8 5TZ, England
Penguin Books USA Inc., 375 Hudson Street, New York, New York 10014, USA
Penguin Books Australia Ltd, Ringwood, Victoria, Australia
Penguin Books Canada Ltd, 10 Alcorn Avenue, Toronto, Ontario, Canada M4V 3B2
Penguin Books (NZ) Ltd, 182–190 Wairau Road, Auckland 10, New Zealand

Penguin Books Ltd, Registered Offices: Harmondsworth, Middlesex, England

First published 1997
1 3 5 7 9 10 8 6 4 2

All pictures supplied by Fortean Picture Library

The moral right of the author has been asserted

Filmset in Monotype Baskerville

Made and printed in England by Clays Ltd, St Ives plc

British Library Cataloguing in Publication Data
A CIP catalogue record for this book is available from the British Library

ISBN 0–140–38585–1

Contents

Is There Anybody There?

It's late, very late. Well past midnight, you guess, though strangely your watch seems to be playing up. Perhaps it got wet when you and your older brother got soaked by the rain on your way over here. There's just the two of you in the old house, the creaky, rattling old place that your grandfather left to you in his will.

Your basic haunted spot: St Mary's Church, Tintern, Gwent.

It seemed like such a good idea, to come over and check it out tonight. But now, with the electricity cut off because of the storm, you're not so sure. The locals gave the pair of you some funny looks when you asked for directions, back in the village. Still, here in the study with the fire crackling in the grate, surrounded by all the dusty old books, it seems safe enough …

Crack! That thunderclap was loud! Made both of you jump. Surely you're not frightened of a creaky old house, are you? Wait: what's that … that … that shuffling noise? Is it the shutters banging again? No, it's nearer: it's in the hallway – just outside this room! Footsteps? Can't be – can it? No, it's just the floorboards creaking, isn't it? It sounds very much like footsteps, large heavy footsteps getting nearer and nearer to the door. Only one thing for it: one of you has got to have a look. Maybe your imagination is just playing tricks – or, at least, that's what you keep telling yourself as your brother pushes you in front of him. Your trembling hand reaches for the doorknob … Then it starts to turn. Somebody – or something – is trying to get in!

We have always loved ghost stories, but what about the ones that appear to be true, the seemingly real encounters between the living and the dead? Have you ever thought, while you were watching *The X-Files* or lying in bed at night listening to the strange clunking noise given off by the central heating, what it would actually be like to be an investigator into this paranormal world? To know the truth behind one of the greatest mysteries of the age: do ghosts exist?

Well, now is your chance, because this book is your guide to being a real-life ghost investigator. So slip on that trusty raincoat, grab your notebook and start investigating. Just keep telling yourself: I ain't afraid of no ghosts …

How to be a Ghost Investigator

So, you want to be an investigator into the world of the paranormal, do you? You may have dreams of being the next Mulder or Scully, but we're sorry to have to tell you that the FBI doesn't usually sign up people as young as yourself to be an agent in their top-secret paranormal investigation division. Also, it has to be said, they prefer them to live in America and to be fully qualified secret agents. Sorry about that.

No problem: it's far easier to be an amateur investigator: there are no horribly complicated entrance exams, for a start. Besides, all those endless reports and other pieces of paperwork that agents have to write seem too much like homework to be fun. Anyway, you know how it is with senior government figures: they're always losing vital evidence or tearing up your reports on 'Orders from Above'. Believe us, you wouldn't want officials like that telling you what to do all the time.

No, stay independent, and your investigations should be able to get that much nearer to the Truth.

Creating your own ghost files

There are two distinct sides to being a ghost investigator. Yes, it's great fun running around seeing ghosts all over the place, having your homework eaten by mischievous poltergeists and getting caught by the ghoulies. But, let's face it, these events are not exactly commonplace. Most of a ghost hunter's time is taken up with assembling data and information, to discover the truth of a case.

Every individual case is known as a File, and each one must stay open until a proper, provable explanation has been found for the events which took place. As you can imagine, many of the classic files remain unexplained to this day. But then, you weren't on the case back then, were you?

Create your own files on ghost cases, collecting every scrap of information you can find. Include witness statements, photographs, drawings, clippings from newspapers and magazines, and so on. The smallest and least significant scrap of evidence may be just what's needed to blow a case wide apart.

Research is the key

A keen investigator should be familiar with all the latest theories about ghosts and their supposed explanations. Obviously you already have the most useful aid to that (this book, stupid). To help expand your investigations, there is also a section on further reading at the end of this book. There are several magazines for spook fanatics, too. Your local library should be able to help track down obscure titles … that is, if the books haven't already been drawn out by a sinister, shadowy figure who turned up just as the clock struck twelve and who has never been seen again!

Read as much as you can on the subject, but don't forget to swot up on hoaxes and frauds just as much as on apparently real encounters. There are many books on ghosts written by people who believe in ghosts no matter what; even when hoaxes are exposed, some so-called experts refuse to admit the Truth. Also, keep one eye open for television news reports and special documentaries on famous cases like Borley Rectory and the Cottingley Fairies. Some will not treat the subject very seriously, but others may well help you close a troublesome file.

In these days of the Internet, the World Wide Web and all the rest, agents have access to the latest high-tech analytical devices. You may be startled to learn that you do too, if you have a home PC. Keep all your records in computer files – but remember to make copies in case some sinister government agency decides to make off with them as part of a cover-up. Separate the files into categories: not just date, time and place, but type of encounter (see page 20), similarities to other cases, and any possible explanations. Look out for patterns!

The Internet is a vital resource for many ghost investigators. Because it cannot be censored, it is home to all kinds of maddo arguments and explanations for super-natural phenomena – but the truth must be out there somewhere. Keep tuned in to the ghost home pages on the World Wide Web for the latest developments; there is a list of Website addresses at the end of this book.

FILE STATUS Various cases in this book are marked with our opinion of their current status. This may be a conclusion such as solved, hoax – or still open and unexplained. As you continue your own investigations, you may be able to solve some of these for yourself! Watch out for the latest news based on reports from government scientists, independent investigations into the paranormal and on the Internet.

Agents in the field

If you are lucky, you may get a chance to investigate an actual haunting for yourself. You must be ready to spring into action at any time. Ghosts don't usually make appointments, even the ones which are meant to pop up again and again in the same place, at the same time every year. Be alert! The same thing applies if you are lucky enough to find yourself out on an organized Ghostwatch.

Luckily, the most important pieces of equipment you will need as an investigator you've already got: they are your brain and your senses. With them you'll be able to make sightings, and possibly to explain them. Get into the habit of keeping your eyes and ears open for anything out of the ordinary. Also, as you will soon discover, there are many fakers and hoaxers around, and even more simple misunderstandings and confusing reports, so investigators will need their wits about them if they are ever to discover the Truth.

You will need equipment with which to record any strange phenomena or paranormal encounters you may have. A dedicated investigator will carry these around with him or her at all times – for you can never predict when something unusual will happen!

A notepad and pens are essential for writing down every last detail, no matter how trivial, and for making sketches and diagrams of what you have seen. If you ever do come across something strange, make a note of everything you see and hear. The smallest, most trivial detail could be vitally important in establishing what has occurred. Make sure your pens work before you set off. If you want to take pencils, don't forget a pencil sharpener and an eraser; your superb ten-second sketch of the headless horseman will look far less impressive with masses of crossings-out all over it.

Use a watch to record the time of any strange occurrence – and note too how long it goes on for. It has been known for some peculiar encounters to have resulted in watches stopping or skipping a few hours, so keep an eye on them. By the way, a watch with a luminous dial or an in-built light is essential if you want to see the time in the dark: check this before you find yourself sitting in a dingy dungeon with a bunch of Romans walking through the walls. A stop-watch feature may prove useful too, but be wary of watches that beep. You don't want everyone yelling at you after you scare them half to death when it chimes the hour.

If you are out with other investigators, it's a good idea to synchronize watches before you start. There'll be enough arguing about whether the ghostly spectre was wearing a blue cape or a grey one, or had a beard or not, without having disputes over the actual time you all saw it.

Ghostwatching gear

When out on the trail of a spook, serious ghost hunters carry all manner of unusual but fiendishly useful items with them. If you ever go on a Ghostwatch, remember the following pieces of essential kit.

Chalk and artist's charcoal are useful for marking walls, furniture or whatever; draw round chair legs and ornaments to find out if a poltergeist has shifted anything. Chalk also comes in handy in powdered form; drop it on the floor and it'll stick to people's shoes, thus telling you if it's them who have been running around making all those spooky noises, not a real ghost at all. Dedicated ghost investigators also use fluorescent powder that glows in infra-red light, but it's a bit pricey and the alternative we tried, sherbet, didn't really glow very much. However, talcum powder, flour or sugar seem to work as well as powdered chalk; leave small patches next to doors and windows and any other place where a faker might pass by.

Professional ghost hunters are also keen on masking-tape and reels of fine cotton thread. They use the tape to seal up doors and windows so nothing truly solid can open them to pass through. The thread they string across entrances and corridors, for the same purpose. This can be handy to detect a fraud but, whatever you do, don't go setting up trip-wires where someone will trip over and hurt themselves.

A ghost investigator must know where they're searching, so a large-scale map of the location will prove invaluable. A compass will help you find your way around or pinpoint the direction that strange humming is coming from.

If you find any ghostly objects, you may need a magnifying glass or pocket microscope to examine them closely. To carry them back to 'the lab' for further study, make sure you have a few transparent envelopes and clean plastic containers with you.

Some investigators suggest carrying a few toys or bright shiny trinkets to leave out in cases of suspected poltergeist infestation. The idea is that the mischievous ghost would rather play with them than fling heavy objects at you. Might be worth a try, if you have enough pockets; at the worst, it will give you something to play with when you get tired of telling each other stupid ghost stories.

High-tech hunting

A camera will come in extra handy for proving or disproving whether you saw something peculiar. If you do carry a camera, you should know how to use it. You'll need the right film for the time of day and weather; taking pictures at night is particularly tricky, worse luck. Use films with fast exposures, to avoid anyone wandering into the shot and causing a ghostly blur. Black-and-white film is often better than colour, as it has the fastest exposure time and can be enhanced more easily than colour to bring out hidden features. A motor-drive will allow several pictures to be taken in quick succession. If you are really flash, you could even use a special 'capacitance switch' that will trigger a camera when it detects motion. Practise whipping out your camera and snapping off a shot that's properly in focus. More importantly, perhaps, you should be able to take a photo without sticking your stupid great thumb over the lens. Also practise taking off the lens cap.

If you ever believe that you have snapped something peculiar, make plenty of copies. Keep the original negatives safe, and never ever hand them over to ghostly shapes at the stroke of midnight. Just as deadly, don't listen to developers who suggest retouching the pictures just a little to really bring out the spooky figure in the background.

If you're lucky, you may have access to a video camcorder. These are even more useful, as they can take many more shots than a regular camera, of course, and can prove whether an object moves. However, they are far more complicated to control and focus, and their picture quality isn't always as good as still film.

Other useful devices can include a small tape recorder, for picking up odd sounds and for dictating your experiences into; walkie-talkies may help you keep in touch with your fellow investigators. Some experts recommend carrying a thermometer, so any temperature changes can be detected and analysed, though a keen investigator like yourself will surely notice if it suddenly grows very cold or very hot.

Truly dedicated ghost hunters have been known to carry all sorts of incredible equipment, including infrared and radar devices, night-vision binoculars, 'environmental monitoring units' (EMUs) that analyse vibrations, air pressure and temperature, and even computers. Such devices are very specialist, however, and may be just a little beyond the range of your pocket money.

What you will need are some tasty snacks, and a flask of something nice to drink will help those long Ghostwatches pass more quickly. And finally … get yourself a huge bag or case in which to carry all this junk, or have a helpful parent with a small truck parked near by.

The Golden Rules for investigations

Now put your hand up in the air and repeat after us … that you will uphold the following Golden Rules at all times.

Look for the truth: Almost everything that people report as a ghostly encounter, whether a spooky noise, a cold spot or a full manifestation complete with head neatly tucked under one arm, can be explained by a perfectly ordinary set of circumstances. It is too easy to go out looking for ghosts and to believe you've had an encounter, precisely because that's what you wanted to see. That insistent knocking may well just be the central heating, but an overactive imagination will have you convinced in no time that it's a restless spectre if you're not very careful.

What ghost investigators are looking for are those very rare encounters which cannot be explained at present and, beyond those, that one golden event which will actually prove the existence of life beyond the grave. Be patient; the Truth is waiting to be found.

When looking for explanations for phenomena, be very wary of weird theories. We still do not know whether or not ghosts even exist. Nothing is certain, nothing is proved. That's why we want you on the case!

Beware of hoaxes: People love to play tricks, particularly on gullible people who believe in ghosts without question or real evidence; so watch out for hoaxes and fakes. Some will be just a piece of harmless fun, a practical joke that got out of hand, but some can genuinely scare sensitive people.

Just as importantly: don't ever be tempted to create a hoax yourself. It may start out seeming like a harmless bit of fun, but matters can always get out of hand. Whether it's hanging a white sheet up in your hallway and taking a photo, or spending months bombarding the next-door neighbours with old coins and water in the hope of convincing them they have a poltergeist for a lodger, just DON'T DO IT.

Be safe: Always tell an adult where you are going; better yet, get one to assist in your investigations. Ask permission first, particularly if, say, you want to stay up all night in your gran's attic waiting for the ghost of Uncle Arthur to show up. Follow all the usual rules about not talking to strangers.

Don't even think about staking out a possible haunted house unless you have permission from a friend or relation who lives there. Don't ever trespass! Better still, go on a properly organized Ghostwatch.

Some people believe so strongly that ghosts don't exist that they think studying them is getting involved with the occult and suchlike. They are entitled to their opinions; all we want to do is to try to tell you as best we can what evidence there is – so you can make up your own mind. Above all, ghost investigating is supposed to be fun, but don't be dim: stay safe.

Ghost Stories

We all love a good spook story. Since the dawn of time, when people huddled nearer to the campfire and tried to ignore the howling of the sabre-toothed tigers or wolves near by, one bright spark has always piped up with a tale of the supernatural. Often the stories had a message: don't be afraid of death, there's something better to follow – or, on the other hand, don't go around killing people because you'll get stuck here as a ghost and won't be allowed to go to the Happy Hunting Grounds with the rest of us. Ghost stories are also told because they are entertainment of the purest sort: rattling good yarns, full of the sort of thrills and chills people have always found scary but fun. You're probably read an R. L. Stine 'Goosebump' book yourself.

To primitive man, the world was alive with beings. He saw the creatures he hunted, running in herds and grazing. But he also saw trees and flowers grow and fall, rivers run fast in spring and slowly in autumn – and he must have thought they were alive. Everything in his world had spirits living alongside the human beings and the animals. Eventually man developed ceremonies and rituals to communicate with these 'spirits', in order to persuade a river to flow faster or the rain to fall. Many cultures believed that, when people died, they too became spirits. Scientists know all this because, in some parts of the world such as Papua New Guinea or the depths of the Amazon, tribes continue to live just as early man did.

As civilizations developed, concerns about death became more elaborate. The Egyptians firmly believed in an afterlife: when important people were buried, models of boats and the statues of friends and guards were included with them to help them on their journey to the Underworld. In many tombs, archaeologists have found fragments of the Egyptian *Book of the Dead*, in essence a guidebook for a departing spirit so that it could reach the other side safely. They were scared that, if a person was not buried and properly assisted, their spirit would end up lost and would roam the earth, causing all sorts of trouble. Some of the earliest ghost stories ever recorded come from these distant times. There is one from about 1200 BC which tells how, some centuries earlier, a high priest of Amon was haunted by the former chief treasurer of King Rehotep. The poor ghost was troubled by the ramshackle state of his tomb. When it was dug up and refurbished, the ghost was laid to rest and haunted no more. Similar tales have been found in the Assyrian and Babylonian cultures, and indeed this fear, that an improper burial would produce a ghost, has continued, through just about every culture of mankind, to this day.

Ancient ghosts

The Greeks believed that, on death, a person's spirit went to heaven, which they called Elysium; but a darker part of the person, which they called the *eidolon* or shade, went to the Underworld. As long as a person's body stayed intact, however, the shade would remain linked to the surface world. If a body wasn't buried or cremated properly, again it was said to wander the earth and to haunt the living. In Homer's epic *Iliad*, the ghost of Patroclus haunts the heroic Achilles, lamenting that he's not been given a proper burial.

In the famous Battle of Marathon in 490 BC, ten thousand Greeks heroically held off an overwhelming force of Persians; the site of the battle was said to be haunted, and ghostly scenes from the bloody conflict were supposedly replayed up to five centuries after it had occurred. (See page 43 for more modern examples of this phenomenon.)

The Romans also firmly believed in ghosts. Each May, every family performed a ceremony called *lemuria*, in which family ghosts were laid to rest so that they would not bother anyone any more. At midnight, the head of the household would walk through the property, leaving behind a trail of black beans to attract any lurking ghost; then he would repeat a special phrase nine times, and the spirits would be banished.

Some of the very best of the early ghost stories come from ancient Rome. In his *Letters*, Pliny the Younger told of a ghostly apparition that haunted the philosopher Athenodorus, who had rented a house in Athens very cheaply. He soon found out why. During the first night he heard a clanking of chains and out shambled the spectre of an old man, thin and filthy, with a long beard and hair that stood on end. The vision beckoned to Athenodorus and led him out into the courtyard, before vanishing. At dawn the next day, the philosopher dug at the spot where the ghost had disappeared and there he found a chained-up skeleton. He immediately had it buried properly, and nobody ever saw the ghost again. This tale, which was probably a shaggy dog story even back then, has reappeared in many forms over the centuries.

The Bible also has its fair share of ghostly encounters. In the Old Testament story of King Saul, the Witch of Endor summoned up the ghost of the prophet Samuel. And there are tales of hauntings by apparitions: the Book of Job describes how the prophet was scared by a ghost in the middle of the night: 'Then a spirit passed before my face; the hair of my flesh stood up. It stood still, but I could not discern the form thereof.'

Eastern ghosts

Ghosts appear in other religious writings as well. For example, there is a Buddhist text which describes how the Buddha trained himself to overcome fear by sitting and meditating at night in a haunted graveyard! The modern Tibetan Buddhist funeral rites include a command to the spirit of the dead person not to haunt the living.

There are hoary old ghost stories similar to Pliny's in Japanese and Chinese mythology. In Eastern cultures, where ancestor worship is strong, ghost stories abound. These days many Chinese people believe in ghosts, somewhat sceptically, knowing they are against the reasoning of modern science but not wishing to discredit the idea entirely. Although it is frowned upon, some Asian cultures even include superstitious ceremonies to appease ghosts, even if (just like many European superstitions such as walking under ladders or pinching and punching on the first of the month) these may not be taken entirely seriously. When people in China are ill, for example, they curse ghosts and demons, the *gwei*, for causing the illness. More dramatically, in Singapore it has been known – if rarely – for two dead people's ghosts to be married to each other by their families so that their younger siblings can marry without breaking the rule that older children must marry first.

Wooh-ooh! A haunting vision from a nineteenth-century book.

European ghosts

While Europeans have rarely gone quite so far to appease the ghosts, at times we have taken quite severe steps to ensure that we can sleep easily at night. There is a great deal of evidence to suggest that our early Celtic and

Viking ancestors went to elaborate lengths to protect themselves against spooks.

For example, in 1835 at Haraldskjaer Fen in Denmark, a body was discovered in a peat bog; it was of a young woman from the Iron Age. When she was buried, she had been tied up and her limbs pinned down with wooden crooks. It was plain that someone was afraid she was going to get up out of her grave after she had been buried! Bodies in a similar condition have been found more recently during other archaeological digs – not often, but certainly often enough to show that it was a genuine fear among the people of that time. And not just back then: a body from the 1360s, dug up at Bocksten, in Holland, had also been pinned down. Furthermore, it had also been buried at a crossroads where four parishes met – shades of vampirism about that one!

Whenever people were writing, some of the stories they told were ghost stories. During the reign of Richard II, a Yorkshire monk illuminating a manuscript filled up the blank pages at the end with his own collection of outlandish ghost stories! And of course, there are plenty of ghosts in Shakespeare's plays, where they are usually a portent of doom!

Despite the spread of Christianity, many folk beliefs and superstitions would not die. Chief among these was a belief in ghosts. In country areas people saw them all the time – of course they existed! Marsh gas has been inspiring tales of will-o'-the-wisps and jack-o'-lanterns for centuries. Nowadays we know that they are flames seen over swampy ground, caused when methane gas, which is produced by rotting vegetation, catches fire and burns until the gas is used up. In earlier times, however, they were thought to be either an evil ghost who wanted to lure people off the path into a treacherous quicksand or a friendly ghost who, if helped, would show the way to fabulous buried treasure! In America, they were explained by the legend of a headless ghost who stalked the marshland searching for his missing part under the light of a blazing lantern.

Despite all the folk myths, by the seventeenth century

No, honest, it's the ghost of dead writer Giuseppe Parini, summoned up by the 'amazing' Carlo Mirabelli (left) in the 1920s.

some people were doing more than telling ghost stories: they were collecting them and analysing their truth or otherwise. In England, a man called Joseph Glanvill collected hundreds, trying to get as much detail as possible so he could determine how true each was.

And as soon as there were ghost investigators, they were finding fakes. Charles Mackay's book *Extraordinary Popular Delusions and the Madness of Crowds* reveals many stories of ghostly trickery. One tale he collected told of six monks who were put up by the King of France in a large house at Chantilly. It was plain, however, that they would have preferred to live in the royal palace. Soon there were reports of strange events at the palace: shrieks, coloured lights, clanking chains in the night and a horrible spectre with a long white beard. The monks announced that they would try to get rid of the diabolical intruders if everyone else moved out. Strangely enough, the haunting stopped when the deeds handing over the castle were signed and sealed.

Slowly but surely, the collection and analysis of ghost stories became more sophisticated. In the mid-nineteenth century, as science began to seek explanations for everything under the sun, some academics turned their attention to the paranormal. In 1851, several students at Cambridge University formed a Ghost Society; it proved so popular that it inspired other groups. Less than twenty years later, these groups combined into the Society for Psychical Research (SPR) – and the modern age of the ghost investigator began.

Spooks, Spectres and Phantoms

The study of ghosts is properly called ghostology. While we're doing the dictionary stuff, 'ghost' is probably from the Middle English word, *gaest*, which means something like 'anger' or 'troubled'. Studying ghosts, as we've seen, has been going on for centuries, but it has always proved troublesome. Perhaps, as a ghost investigator you will be able to cut through much of the confusion and nonsense surrounding the subject.

One of the things you will notice when you compile your files is that, while people love telling ghost stories, they are in the habit of changing them or leaving bits out if it makes the story better! Supposedly serious studies of classic ghost cases often propose all kinds of dubious evidence, claiming it all to be true. Many ages-old cases are presented as new events. Tales which scholars have known to be urban myths for decades suddenly crop up as 'true stories'.

Worse, loads of reports get so far – you know: 'The police left, baffled, saying there was nothing they could do' – and then the story ends, dead! Stories like this will leave you shouting at the page: what happened next? Is it still going on, twenty years later, or did the ghost just push off again when the papers stopped writing about it? Names and fine details also get changed – though, to be fair, sometimes this is done to protect witnesses who are highly embarrassed that people may think they are the sort of weirdo who sees ghosts everywhere! That doesn't exactly help the amateur ghost investigator – but we trust someone as keen as you will get through to the Truth!

The very worst source of confusion about ghost investigating, though, is when one comes to pin down what a ghost actually is!

Movie ghosts

What a ghost 'should' look like; St. Mary's churchyard, Prestbury, 1990.

Or perhaps that heading should be 'Scooby Doo Ghosts'. Because we all know what a ghost looks like, don't we? We've all seen TV shows, cartoons and films, and we've all read stories and comic strips featuring ghosts. Of course, there are always exceptions: *The X-Files*, the creepy stories of M. R. James or Peter Straub, say. But most of the time it's the same old story.

A 'movie ghost', as we all know, looks like a sheet with eye-holes cut in it – like the easiest costume a kid can make at Hallowe'en. Of course, as film special effects have got better, this classic look has become more sophisticated. Computer-generated ghosts like Casper are more transparent these days, though they are still little more than animated bed-sheets. And as that lovable spook shows us, he can go through walls, pick up objects or people – and talk!

If it's not a sheet with eyes, it's a man or woman in Elizabethan costume with their head stuck under their arm, strolling around a draughty old castle in England. They often turn up in comedy shows, because there's always room for 'hilarious consequences', with the head taking on a life of its own.

Well, forget all that.

Proper ghosts

'Real' ghosts – that is, ghosts which people have reported often enough for investigators to study properly – are very different from the clichés. For one thing, they aren't see-through. The most common complaint by witnesses to ghostly visitations is that they were totally unaware they were in the presence of a dead person until the ghost disappeared again! Ghosts generally act and look just like any living person and are usually not identified as a spook until long into their appearance, or even afterwards, when information is discovered indicating that the person seen was dead. Indeed, some psychic researchers suggest that this may mean we are all seeing many ghosts all the time – without ever knowing it!

All this is assuming that the ghost is in human form. Poltergeists are never seen; other types of ghost manifest as sounds or strange odours, or merely as 'presences'. There are many reports of ghostly animals of all types – including some very unusual species. Haunted vehicles have included buses, cars, motorbikes, ships and aircraft. Further ghosts are said to be attached to old objects – but we guess that a haunted armchair or a headless duck (see later!) just wouldn't scare moviegoers as much as a maniac in a hockey mask.

That's another myth which should be dispelled. There is little evidence that ghosts are out to kill or harm anybody. It must be admitted that people with weak hearts have been scared to death by what they thought were ghosts, but they were not physically harmed. Even poltergeists, despite making a nuisance of themselves by throwing objects around suburban living-rooms, always seem to be trying to miss; people get hurt only by accident. Hardly the avenging demons popular myth would have you believe in.

Ghosts are seen in many places, not just in empty, tumbledown old houses handily situated at the top of a desolate hill or in a crumbling but stately castle. New homes are just as likely to be haunted – as are theatres and cinemas, banks, bus stops, stretches of motorway, ancient woodlands, caves, public toilets and so on. Wherever people are, it's odds-on there will be a ghost along sooner or later.

For a keen ghost investigator, a report that a ghost fits into one or more of the old clichés should be a clear sign that the report is more than likely a fake or merely wishful thinking. Know your stuff, and you'll soon separate the hoaxes from the genuine cases.

Spooky encounters

In order to study ghosts, you need to know what you are looking for. To this end, we will be dividing into four categories the sorts of phenomena you may find yourself investigating – sort of Spooky Encounters of the First to Fourth Kind. The gaps between the categories aren't always clear-cut, and many cases will appear to have aspects of more than one type, for example, a ghost that appears but which also knocks and raps like a poltergeist. Ghost hunters sometimes use other categories, based on different resoning, but these are clear and easy to apply to an encounter:

1) Crisis Apparition
The image of a loved one or friend who turns up to announce their death, often at the time it happens and across a wide distance. One-off events, usually, so they are very hard to study in any really scientific way. Also more specialized forms, such as living ghosts and the terrifying doppelgängers.

2) Recording Ghost
An apparition (whether an image, a sound, or whatever — or a combination) that seems tied to a specific location, as if it were a recording of a person that keeps on being played long after their death. In more extreme forms, may be a time-slip.

3) Haunting Ghost
The real thing, a ghost that interacts with those who see or hear it, responding to them just like a living person. May be a human, an animal or even, occasionally, an inanimate object!

4) Poltergeist
Possibly not a ghost at all! A crazy force that throws objects around, causes items to appear and devices to behave oddly; may be a spirit or just a wild external sign of emotional frustration coming from a human being.

Crisis Apparitions

In December 1918, two pilots set off to fly from Scampton airfield in Lincolnshire to Tadcaster in Yorkshire. One pilot was delivering a new plane; the other was bringing along a second craft to ferry his comrade back home again. Some way into their journey, the two pilots ran into very thick cloud and fog which made flying very dangerous. The second plane made a forced landing, but the pilot of the first one pressed on, anxious to complete his job. At 3.25 p.m., less than a kilometre from

Tadcaster, the first pilot, Lieutenant David McConnel, was killed when his plane crashed. Meanwhile, back at Scampton, McConnel's friend, Lieutenant James Larkin, was writing some letters in their barrack-room when his comrade clattered through the doorway in his usual fashion and entered the room, greeting Larkin as always with a cheery 'Hello, boy!' He was dressed in full flying gear, with his old naval cap perched jauntily on his head. He was smiling as usual. Larkin was surprised to see him back so early, but McConnel told him, 'Yes, got there all right. Had a good trip.' After a moment, the man bade his friend farewell and left as noisily as he had arrived. He was never seen again. It was only later, on hearing the terrible news of McConnel's fatal crash at around 3.25 p.m., that Larkin worked out that he had seen 'McConnel' a little while before half-past three.

Cue the spooky music! That's a classic case of a Crisis Apparition, the appearance of a friend or relation in front of someone at the very moment of their death, often from a great distance away. It's among the most commonly reported of all ghostly phenomena, and one that has been recorded since serious ghost investigating began.

Because there are so many casualties during wartime, many Crisis Apparitions are reported during such conflicts. One wonders whether the pressure of having a loved one serving so far away and in such danger somehow makes the ghost's witness much more open to the phenomenon.

Here's another famous example. On 19th March 1917, a young Englishwoman living in India was playing with her baby when she looked up and was startled but overjoyed to see her brother standing in the doorway. He was an airman who had been fighting in France. She turned to put her baby down but, when she turned back to greet him, there was no sign of him. She called his name again and again, and then she searched the entire house from top to bottom but there was no sign of him, and no one else had seen him. Eventually she had to admit that he had not really been there. Two weeks later an official letter arrived, carrying the terrible news that her brother had been shot down and killed while flying over the Western Front – on 19th March 1917!

Of course, Crisis Apparitions have also been recorded during peacetime. In fact, if you start asking around, you will discover that a great many families have stories of how a dear departed relation turned up to startle his widow or a relative. Maybe a tale of just such an appearance occurs in your own family. Typically, such tales gather their own momentum, growing in the telling, and they get so distorted that they are hard to study. They become a small-scale version of an urban myth, a false story that people swear happened to someone they know but which turns out to be always lacking in any details or evidence. As you might guess correctly, this will make such tales very hard to study or explain in any meaningful way.

It isn't just members of a family who materialize; friends and associates can also make a farewell appearance in the form of a Crisis Apparition. One woman even had the image of her long-serving cleaning-woman turn up. Of course, if it's only a friend or an acquaintance who turns up, it may be the case that someone saw 'something', and only later, on hearing of a friend's untimely passing, jumped to the conclusion (rightly or wrongly) that it was the ghost of this person that they saw.

For example, in California in October 1976, Mrs Berger was asleep in her bed when she woke up with a start. Peering through her open bedroom door, she could see across the hall into her living-room. There she saw the shape of a woman, dressed in a long green robe or caftan. The face was hazy and she did not recognize her. In panic, thinking it was a burglar, Mrs Berger called out and turned on her bedroom light. The figure faded away. After searching the apartment and finding nothing out of order, Mrs Berger settled back into bed and turned out the light – and the figure was there again. This time she turned on the lights and kept them on. The next day, she had a sad call telling her that a close friend had died the night before. It was only when she put the phone down that Mrs Berger remembered that her late friend often wore a long green caftan.

Sometimes the Crisis Apparition seems to bend the laws of reality even further, allowing impossible things to happen in order to get his or her message across. And these days, with modern communications so easy to use, some Crisis Apparitions don't even turn up 'in person' at all. In the early 1980s, a woman in Cheshire was doing the ironing. The telephone rang and she picked it up, to hear her husband saying in a strange voice, 'I am very far away.' As his voice faded away, she realized she was clutching thin air – because the couple didn't have a telephone! A few hours later, when the police arrived, she was told he had been killed by someone trying to steal their car; he must have died around the same time as his ghostly call came through.

Crisis Apparitions seem to manifest in two specific ways. A number appear in the form they are in at the time of the crisis: someone in a car cash may by lying at an odd angle for example. Thankfully, however, such horrific ghosts are rare. The majority present themselves as though nothing were wrong. Although they may not interact properly with a witness, they stand, walk or sit as though they were a living and breathing person.

Some theories

The Crisis Apparition is the form of ghost which presents the greatest problems for the eager young ghost investigator. For a start, most of them are witnessed by only one person, or (very rarely) by two or more members of the same family. Furthermore, they turn up just the once, at the moment the crisis occurs; after that, they are never seen again. Piling round to a Crisis Apparition witness's house with all your ghost-hunting gear is not going to turn up any further clues at all.

This all means that reports of Crisis Apparitions rely solely on the word of the witness. Since they result from the death of someone close to the witness, it's impossible to discount the fact that they might just be wishful thinking, little more than a fantasy brought about by grief and remembered later. We all dream about our friends and family, as well as about imaginary people. If one dreamed about a friend and then received the shocking news that they had died tragically, it would not be too hard to convince oneself that they had turned up – why, it must have been right at the moment they were passing away.

More fanciful are those theories suggested by people who firmly believe that such visions are of dead people's spirits. Some think these apparitions are 'passing callers' – it's the spirit of the dearly departed popping in to say one last goodbye on their way to heaven or the other place. It's a nice idea, but it bears more relation to a fairy tale than to any scientific explanation. Several films and books have taken this theory as their plot; it's an oft-used theme.

A little more rationally, some researchers have suggested that they are the end result of a form of energy which is given out at the traumatic moment, like a huge flash of power. This is then transmitted to someone who can receive it – specifically, someone so close to the 'transmitter' that they can pick up the final message. How this actually happens is not explained, of course – science has not yet proved the existence of telepathy or ESP, if indeed it ever will.

It is hard to determine from cases of Crisis Apparitions when the ghost in fact turned up. If it was before they died, some have suggested that this was a desperate cry for help; if during the event, maybe it was one last massive psychic scream that can only be 'heard' by those most sensitive to the person. If the apparition is actually seen after his or her death, that is less likely to be an option.

Crisis Apparitions are peculiar phenomena. To the people who experience them they seem genuine enough, for the most part, but who knows how much is down to the mind playing tricks, especially under the influences of grief?

FILE STATUS

Unexplained and hard to study.

Casebook: The London ghost bus

A very strange case, related to Crisis Apparitions, is that of the ghost bus of North Kensington. In the mid-1930s there was a dangerously sharp corner that was the cause of several traffic accidents. Local residents started reported sightings of a ghostly bus. At first, when they complained to the local bus depot, they didn't realize that it was a phantom: one of the company's vehicles, they said, had been seen hurtling round that corner in the early hours of the morning. Witnesses began to admit that the bus they had seen had its headlights full on; however, although its inside lights were also on, there was no sign of any crew or passengers. The bus had caused several accidents, including one fatal car crash when a vehicle swerved out of its path and hit a wall. The bus company really started taking the matter seriously when an inspector, at work very early one morning, saw a bus draw up (long before any buses were due out), stand with its engine running for a few seconds, then disappear!

Some researchers have speculated that the bus was an emotional projection formed by local people. Their concerns about the dangerous corner had manifested themselves as the ghostly bus which caused even more accidents. Who knows? What is certain is that, when the corner was smoothed out, the ghost bus was never seen again!

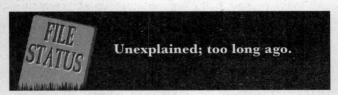

FILE STATUS   Unexplained; too long ago.

Living Ghosts

Crisis Apparitions are one thing – but what would you do if the apparition of someone plainly still living turned up? Writing in his autobiography, the famous Irish poet W. B. Yeats tells how one afternoon, back when he was a student at the end of the last century, he had a message he wanted to give to a friend in another part of the country. Two days after that, he was surprised to receive a letter from this fellow student, answering the message Yeats hadn't yet sent! The previous afternoon, the letter said, Yeats had suddenly appeared in the middle of a group of people in a hotel, as solid as anyone. His friend had seen him, but no one else had; the student, frightened, had told him to come back when everyone else had gone. Later that night, Yeats had apparently done just that, and had passed on the message!

When the Society for Psychical Research did a survey of Crisis Apparitions, as many people reported seeing living people as dead ones. Of course, we all see living people – but not living people who aren't really there, people who at the moment they are seen are in another town or another country.

Just as with Crisis Apparitions of the dead, such apparitions often seem to be associated with times of great stress. There was the case of a man who, working in his garden one day, saw a friend walk past his house. He greeted her but was surprised when she did not reply but just kept on walking. He thought he must have been mistaken – but it did look awfully like her, and he was certainly close enough to see. Later that day he rang her to ask if everything was all right. He discovered her at home, as she had been all day. She was alive but very unhappy, and in fact it turned out she was starting a full nervous breakdown. Such emotional trauma seems to have sent her image to appear to her friend – though what it was trying to convey by walking past his house is anyone's guess!

In a few reported cases the living apparition does not appear far away, but instead is seen in his or her own home, where one might well expect them to be. In 1983, the writer Ted Simon had gone with his wife and son to visit one of his mother's friends, an elderly widow who lived near Southend. When they arrived, her house lights were all on, so he rang the doorbell several times. Getting no answer, he peered in through the window and saw her dodder over from the kitchen and cross her living-room in the direction of the front door. He couldn't see her face but, from her walk and shape, it was her all right. However, she didn't answer the door. He rang again and again, but nobody came. This time when he looked there was nobody inside. He called through the letterbox, then he went and found a phone box and rang the house, but there was no answer. The next day, back at home, when he tried ringing again, he got through to the old widow – who told him she had been away at her daughter's house. The lights had been left on to dissuade burglars. So what had Mr Simon seen?

Just like regular Crisis Apparitions, these ghosts are hard to study, even for the keenest investigators; they do not hang around long enough, for a start. One thing's for certain – they are not ghosts, as such, because the people they depict are not dead!

So we must consider other explanations. A believer might suggest ESP or some other form of thought transference, though proving this is extremely hard to do at present. Again, some of these apparitions seem to be conjured up at times of stress, though by no means all of them. Further investigation is plainly called for.

Alternatively, a sceptic would say that they are all merely hallucinations generated by the mind's eye of the beholder, delusions caused by a combination of wishful thinking and fantasy. One famous case has a great bearing on such matters. Dr Morton Schatzman, an eminent London psychiatrist, reported the case of an American woman living in Britain, whom he called 'Ruth'. She was experiencing frequent apparitions, not of a dead person, but mainly of her father, who she knew was alive and perfectly well back in the States. Rather than try to stop her having them, Schatzman helped her to create and then learn to control them, by concentrating upon them. After some effort, she could create lifelike, three-dimensional images in her brain. Most of the time she could do it to order, and she even produced a phantom Dr Schatzman. Devices wired to her brain waves showed that, although the images were not real, she seemed to see them so strongly that they imposed themselves between the signals going from her eyes towards her brain. What she was seeing were undeniably hallucinations, but she had so much control over their creation that this case may provide clues to explain what other less sensitive people are seeing as well.

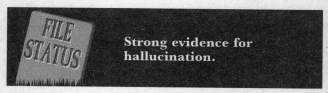

FILE STATUS

Strong evidence for hallucination.

Seeing double

As we've already said, as many people reported seeing Crisis Apparitions of living people as of dead ones. There is one type of living ghost, however, that turns up very rarely indeed – for which we should all be very thankful. This is the doppelgänger. It's a German word, and it really just means someone's double. For these are the peculiar cases of people who have met themselves!

Adrian Brown worked for a security firm in Winton, Dorset. As reported in the *Dorset and Poole Advertiser*, in 1990 his job was to drive around a number of sites in a company van, checking that everything was safe and secure. Usually he was able to keep to a strict timetable, but on one particular night a problem had delayed him for twenty minutes. Now he was on his way to a gravel pit, but upon reaching a roundabout near Holton Heath he saw a shocking sight. Lit up in a lorry's headlights, coming back the other way, was a white van identical to the one he was driving. As it passed him, the driver turned his head to glance at him – and Mr Brown found himself looking at himself! After this, the poor man drove on, checked the gravel pit and then headed for home, deeply shaken. Trying to find an explanation for what he had seen, he wondered whether he had seen the company's other van, but he knew that it had broken down and was off the road that day. Then he realized that the duplicate van and its ghostly driver were just where he would have been, had he not been twenty minutes late!

There is a hint in Mr Brown's story that the possible cause could have been, not a ghost, but a time-slip. This situation occurs when a person seems to slip backwards or forwards in time, and witnesses events or scenes from the past or the future. We will examine the phenomenon in full later (see page 49), but consider this case as well.

The famous German writer Goethe tells in his autobiography how he was out riding his horse one day when he began to feel very peculiar. Coming back towards him, also riding a horse and wearing a grey suit with gold trim, was himself. Eight years later, he says, he happened to find himself riding along the same lane, but in the opposite direction. In a flash he remembered the previous incident and realized that he was actually wearing a grey suit with gold trim. On this occasion, however, he did not meet his unearthly doppelgänger. Again, this lends at least some substance to a 'time-slip' explanation.

Other incidents, however, are of a more domestic nature and are far harder to unravel. Take the case of a woman, a recent widow, who was having trouble sleeping. In the early hours of one December morning in 1992, she rolled over in bed to find a woman, dressed in a coat and hat, standing next to the bed and looking down at her. She leapt up with a start – because it was herself! Next to her, her young son, sleeping in the bed with her that night, started to cry in alarm. She turned to comfort him and, when she looked back, the doppel-gänger was gone …

That's all very well. We know it's impossible for us to come face to face with ourselves – which means that, to a large extent, we can put any such apparitions down to hallucination. We've been working too hard and should take a holiday, or perhaps we shouldn't have had that cheese sandwich before we went to bed.

But there are some cases which are guaranteed to turn the most rational person into a quivering paranoid wreck. There was a man, an operating theatre assistant at Westminster Hospital. One day in 1988 he found himself helping an anaesthetist prepare a boy for surgery. As the anaesthetist had to pop out for a moment, he told the lad to ask the assistant to tell him all about being in the Foreign Legion. Puzzled, the assistant later asked the anaesthetist what he had meant by that; the man told him that the last time the pair worked together, the assistant had told a whole lot of tales about being in the Foreign Legion, from which he had eventually managed to escape. None of it was true – indeed, the assistant had never met the doctor before! Looking into the matter, he discovered that it had been his day off when the meeting was alleged to have happened. Someone just like him, it seemed, had been coming in to work and doing his job! Eeek!

The problem, again, with trying to study doppel-gängers is that they don't turn up to order. A theory exists that tries to explain other types of ghosts: it insists that we all have 'etheric doubles', ghostly spirits like souls that are released to wander the earth when we die. Doppelgängers, it follows, are merely those etheric doubles which have come loose and are wandering about already. Ahem. We'll come back to such matters in later sections, but really! No wonder sceptical people put them down to hallucinations – well, if you saw yourself walking towards you along a school corridor, wouldn't you think you were seeing things? On the other hand, having a doppelgänger might come in very handy on those sunny summer mornings when Double

Maths followed by Double Physics is the last thing you want to do.

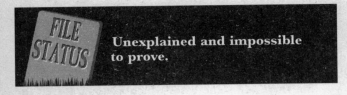

FILE STATUS Unexplained and impossible to prove.

Recording Ghosts

A ghostly apparition that pops up once, for one person, and then disappears again, never to return, is a real pain to study. Take heart, fearless investigator, for the next category of spook is much easier to come across.

Recording Ghosts may turn up again and again, always in the same place and sometimes at the same time each year or decade. Such ghosts may be seen or heard by many people, though most often they are attached to a location rather than to a person. These ghosts are likely to be the first type of ghost or apparition to be explained and understood properly – and such theories may have nothing to do with a spirit coming back from the grave.

A typical Recording Ghost appears as a historical personage, often a former resident of the location where they are seen. They may sit, stand or walk about, but their behaviour will be limited and will be repeated if they turn up on future occasions. Some apparitions, although they may appear to be fully human, may act more like robots or sleepwalkers than fully functioning people. Such ghosts will show no interest in anything around them from the modern world: indeed, they will not interact in any way with anyone or anything round them. On many occasions, in fact, the ghost will respond to some unseen landscape round them – the world as it

A ghostly figure, unusually snapped in daylight, at Alton Church, Staffs, 1993.

was when they were alive. For example, this could mean that their legs are missing from the knees down – because the ancient floor they are allegedly standing on is below the current floor level!

All of this goes to explain why such entities are called Recording Ghosts. It is suggested that they are not animate spirits at all. Far from being an unearthly spirit doomed to wander the world as penance for not having had a proper burial, such apparitions are perhaps some form of supernatural hologram or video recording.

Maybe they were imprinted somehow into the location because of some emotional crisis, and they are being played back for witnesses to experience by some process we don't yet understand. Yes, there are a lot of 'maybes' and 'somehows' in all that. Let's take a closer look.

Seeing ghosts

All of the above is not intended to give the impression that all Recording Ghosts are the same. Many manifestations can be heard, smelt or felt rather than seen, or they may appeal to a combination of senses. For starters, however, we'll examine the basic apparition.

Since Recording Ghosts seem to be tied to a specific location, they are often what you might call 'historical ghosts', that is, they are the image of some figure from the past, whether a Roman soldier, an Elizabethan lady or a Victorian child. Such phantoms are usually former inhabitants of the location, though there are plenty of opportunities for wild guesswork in such deductions. It often happens that, when people think they have seen such a ghost, they will then look back through the annals (or, more likely, be told a daft local legend by some crusty old farmer or wrinkled retainer) and immediately deduce that the person from the legend is what they must have seen. This applies especially to ghosts of recognizable historical figures. For example, the White House in America is home to a tall ghost who many witnesses swear is that of Abraham Lincoln; he has even been seen by people you would consider level-headed, including Sir Winston Churchill and President John F. Kennedy.

This can also work in reverse, continuing to feed back into the legend. For example, one night on a Ghostwatch you think you saw a vague shape, indistinct but apparently dressed in a long, featureless grey robe. Next day you are told that the site of your vigil was an old nunnery, whose inhabitants were murdered. Soon you'll be believing that you were an actual, honest-to-goodness witness privileged to see a rare manifestation of the spooky Sister Immaculata, who was murdered in the fifteenth century.

A hundred years ago, Mrs Eleanor Sidgwick of the SPR noted that most ghosts were seen on glancing around or on suddenly looking up. She was right: even today there appear to be few cases when an apparition pops out while someone is looking directly at the spot where it appears. So many witnesses describe seeing apparitions 'out of the corner of their eye'; it's no wonder people start accusing them of seeing things.

Ghosts witnessed in such a fashion have a tendency to be transparent, floating things. We already know that such apparitions have a pretty good chance of being hallucinations or wishful thinking. Among the most common ghosts is the Grey Lady, a woman with an indistinct face, dressed in a long flowing dress or cloak; there are variants in different colours, but the form tends to stay the same. For example, there was the Grey Lady seen by Lady Carson at Cleve Court, Minster, Kent, in December 1949. Woken in the early hours by her spaniel wanting to be let out, she opened the bedroom door. Her pet scurried out then ran back, whimpering. Down in the hall, Lady Carson saw a young-looking woman in a full-length grey skirt and cape with white lace headgear. She looked alive and walked rather than floated, but without making a sound, then she passed into the Elizabethan part of the house.

Ghostly figures which truly defy analysis and which go some way to presenting a real case for their existence are always much more solid. In short, 'real' ghosts are the sort of figures whom people have greeted or swerved to avoid on a country road, and they are always startled when the figure disappears again. There was the case of a man, an out-and-out sceptic, who was on a Ghostwatch in an allegedly haunted building. He greeted a woman who he thought was another member of the team to whom he hadn't been introduced – and he yelled his head off when she faded away in front of his outstretched hand.

Ghostly monks and nuns seen by witnesses seem to be uncommonly frequent. This could be, believers say, because their lives were governed by timetables: they would always be walking a set path at a set time, for

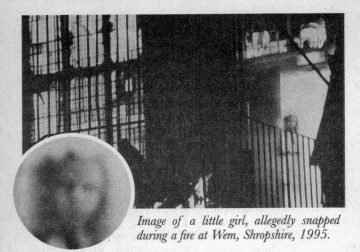

Image of a little girl, allegedly snapped during a fire at Wem, Shropshire, 1995.

example. On the other hand, their robes are also long and flowing, and they tend towards the featureless. See the directory of British ghost sites that starts on page 100 for the locations of many dozens of ghostly monks, nuns, grey ladies, brown ladies, white ladies and so on, that you may even be able to go and see for yourself.

This is not to say that all such ghosts are adults – far from it. Many apparitions, from famous historical young-sters like Lady Jane Grey and the two princes who died in the Tower of London, to unknown tots, seem to pop back as ghosts. One famous case of recent years is the photo of a little girl taken during the fire at Wem town hall. At the height of the blaze, amateur photographer Tony O'Rahilly took a snap from the road opposite. When it was developed four months later, it seemed to show a little girl standing in the doorway of a fire-escape. Upon seeing it, some local historian suggested that it was the ghost of a girl who allegedly started the Great Fire of Wem which all but destroyed the small market town in 1677. Others simply thought it was all a fake. Since the fire, by the way, workmen refurbishing the town hall have reported seeing a ghostly child ... but then they would, wouldn't they?

Casebook: Romans through the wall

Possibly the most famous Recording Ghosts ever seen were those which scared a young apprentice plumber half to death one day in 1953. Harry Martindale is a retired policeman these days, but back then he was helping his boss install central heating in the old Treasurer's House, in historic York. He was up a short ladder, knocking a hole in the cellar ceiling for some pipes to go through; he was alone, save for the lamp he had brought with him. Suddenly he heard the sound of a trumpet call but thought someone upstairs had turned a radio on loudly. However, a few moments later a Roman soldier carrying a long, battered horn marched straight through the wall, closely followed by another on a big carthorse, then a whole column of twenty or so. Harry stepped back in alarm and fell off the ladder, then he scuttled back into the corner of the cellar in fright.

The soldiers were all dressed in identical fashion, each with a helmet on his head. On their upper bodies they wore broad leather bands joined to form a jerkin, above a skirt. Each carried a short sword and many had spears, but only one had a shield, with a raised boss in the middle. They weren't in formation and they looked tired; all were unshaven, many with full beards. They looked nothing like Romans Harry had seen at the movies. Every figure he saw appeared to be a solid, real human being, except that their legs faded into the floor, until they marched across a hole that led down to the level of a Roman road, the Via Decumana, that runs under the building. When they got to that point Harry could see their calves and feet walking on the lower level. When the soldiers reached the other side of the cellar, they disappeared into the wall.

After they had gone, Harry rushed upstairs in a state of shock. He ran into the curator of the Treasurer's House, who immediately said, 'By the look of you, you've seen the Romans, haven't you?' At the curator's request Harry wrote down as much as he could remember. Then

The Roman-haunted Treasurer's House, York.

the curator showed him many other reports, from 1947 and 1933 and even earlier. Furthermore, after Harry's incident there was a second sighting, in 1957, but this one was reported only in 1974 when Harry's own tale slipped out and was made public. Since the 1950s, scholars have pieced together much more information about who the soldiers may have been – though again one has to be wary of jumping to conclusions. So did Harry see ghosts? Well, he was working on his own, in a precarious position in a dark and dingy cellar, lit by a single light, and he knew of the Roman remains all round him. On the other hand, his details closely match the reality of Roman life in Britain, rather than a Hollywoodized version. The jury is still out.

FILE STATUS As an expert said, he was either 'seriously hallucinating, seriously lying, or seriously telling the truth'.

Smelling ghosts

Research by paranormal investigators has shown that around five per cent of cases of Recording Ghosts involve peculiar odours. One which did was reported by a retired NHS psychiatrist, Dr James Gordon-Russell, from Bristol. During a week's holiday in 1967, spent with his family, he was staying in one wing of an old house in North Devon. During the night the youngest child, usually a peaceful baby, wouldn't stop crying. Later, the doctor woke suddenly in his bedroom and smelt a terrible stench, like 'rotting leaves or a graveyard'. The temperature suddenly plunged and then the bedclothes were whisked off the bed. The next day the owner confirmed that others had had similar experiences in the same room, but what it meant he did not know. Nor do we, to be honest.

Not all ghostly pongs are so nasty. Bovey House in Devon, for example, is haunted by a tall but headless lady dressed in a fine blue gown; her presence is always preceded by the heady scent of lavender. Less historically, some people have reported all kinds of ghostly smells that are very mundane – it's just that they don't seem to have a source that can be explained properly. One researcher tells of an actress who believed her flat in Birkenhead was haunted because of phantom cooking smells which invaded the building at inappropriate moments.

The difficulty with such cases is judging just what can be 'explained properly'. A great many people live in houses in which they can, on occasions, tell what the neighbours are having for dinner, since they can smell it as clearly as if it were coming from their own kitchen. Smells are like sounds, but they are even more pervasive: they creep and sneak through cracks in walls and along flues and pipes, and can be transmitted over a surprising distance. Smells also hang around for a long time if left undisturbed; a visitor to a stately home wearing a strong perfume could leave a cloud that might well still be there at 4 a.m. the next morning.

Feeling ghosts

Very few Recording Ghosts have been known to touch
people – and in any case, to be honest, that would be too
much interaction for a proper spook of this type.
However, many encounters come in the form of sudden
and unnatural temperature drops or patches where
strange, emotional lurches are felt (it's like the temperature's dropped, only one feels it inside, they say). Such
patches are known as 'cold spots' and, while they are
often the accompaniment to more obvious apparitions,
they are also known to manifest on their own. Of course,
a sceptic might argue, if you were sitting all night in a
windowless castle, you'd be cold too – and what happens
when we feel frightened? Right, we get goosebumps and
feel shivery. Hmmm. In reply, a less scornful investigator
would already have dismissed the obviously natural
causes; the weird ones might be where the temperature
drops in an instant, or a spot in the corner of a room is
supernaturally spooky all the time.

One very strange and unnatural 'cold spot' was experienced by a young officer-cadet on a Merchant Navy vessel off Ireland in about 1920. At one point in the voyage,
for maybe half a minute, he, the Captain and the Chief
Mate all felt extremely depressed and ill. It was only later
that they realized (or possibly decided) that this was the
point when the ship was directly above the spot where the
Lusitania had been torpedoed in 1915, going down with
the loss of all hands – and all the bodies were still on
board.

There are people who like to think they are 'sensitive'
to the spirits, shall we say, who believe they can tell
whether a house is haunted or not. More commonly,
many everyday people often say that someone's home is a
happy one. We found a file on a woman who, having
moved into an old house in Highgate, London, in the
1970s, picked up its sombre mood. She tried to fight it by
repainting the place in bright colours, but this did not
help. Eventually, one night she awoke sensing that someone was there. At foot of her bed was a woman in

old-fashioned dress, her hair in a bun. She looked sad, almost hopeless. Research turned up the tale of a wife whose husband had died; she was so grief-stricken that she had locked herself in the bedroom until she herself died. (Irritatingly, yet again, we have no further details.)

Hearing ghosts

If odours and cold spots are uncommon, spooky sounds are the opposite. From ghostly footsteps and ominous creaks to full-scale sonic re-creations of historical battles, some ghosts are a right noisy lot! However, despite what horror films may tell you, there are precious few spooks who resort to the classic 'Wooo! Woo!' noises. This seems to have stemmed from a mix-up in people's minds between the ghost and the banshee, the wailing spirit from Irish folklore.

Footsteps are perhaps the most common Recording Ghosts sounds. Not particularly creepy, you might think – but in these cases people have investigated and found tales of footsteps made by invisible feet. In the cellar of an old jeweller's shop in Chester a few years ago, for example, ghost hunter Jenny Randles heard tell of 'George'. That was the pet name the staff had given to their ghost. They'd never seen him, but they had certainly heard him, his footsteps ringing as he climbed a stone staircase that was no longer there. Ms Randles's researches turned up the fascinating information that the building had been constructed on the site of an old jail. The stone steps the staff were hearing led up from the condemned cell to the hangman's noose! If it was emotional stress that imprinted this particular ghostly sound, all we can say is, it's not surprising!

Of course many spook sounds, from clanks and rattles to creaks and footsteps, have perfectly rational explanations. As they expand in the sun, wooden boards move and creak; as they shift they may free up other boards, allowing them to move and creak in turn. Slowly but surely, the noises can cross a floor rather like footsteps. Meanwhile, old central heating will knock and bang as the air that's leaked in hits the water being pumped through it. These days there are also thermostats turning boilers on and off, and fridges that hum and grind at all hours of the day or night. One family, terrified by a high-pitched whistling that scared the living daylights out of them when they moved into an old house in Maryland, in the USA, discovered that someone had stuck a child's whistle between two roofing tiles; every time the wind blew in a certain direction, it gave out the most haunting sounds that echoed round the eaves.

People have heard ghostly noises out of doors too. A ghostly chanting, as if by long-dead monks, is often to be heard at Beaulieu Abbey in Hampshire. More recently, a number of locations both here and in the USA have been plagued with loud humming noises. At Hueytown in Alabama, the loud whining hum that emanates from the surrounding hills seemed to be coming from the enor-mous ventilation fans serving nearby mines. Other cases in Britain have put the blame squarely on gas being pumped down underground pipes.

Animals were behind the Legend of Showman's Rest. In Chicago in 1918 a train crash occurred involving a cir-cus train; more than sixty people were killed, along with numerous animals. Over the years, people had reported hearing ghostly animal noises at the site. The case was solved by a policeman, Sergeant John O'Rourke. Hearing the spooky noises while out on his beat one night, he worked out that he was hearing the sounds of distant Brookfield Zoo, two kilometres away, carried on the still night air.

Drowned villages

We are moving into the realm of folklore here, but there are certainly plenty of tales of phantom noises that are said to come from drowned villages. Around many parts of the European coastline, old settlements have been reclaimed by the waves. The once-thriving port of Dunwich in Suffolk is now a tiny village; the rest is under the waves. Now there are legends that the drowned church bells will ring to warn of impending storms. Similar stories are told about places like South Hayling in Hampshire and Bosham in West Sussex – and also of lost communities said to lie under lakes like Llangorse, near Brecon in Wales. To a sceptical modern eye it's obvious, perhaps, that these have grown up as a mixture of wishful thinking, tales that grew into legends and a need to explain the way spooky sounds can be carried across water at night.

The clamour of battle

Some theories as to how ghosts form suggest that emotional images are somehow stored, almost burnt into the world by an excess of emotion. It's no wonder, then, that there have been many reports of ghostly battles being reenacted on old battlegrounds around the world.

We've already heard how the Greek site of the Battle of Marathon was thought to be haunted. In Britain, the Battle of Edgehill was fought first in October 1642 – and again towards Christmas, if the story is true. Three thousand people died at the battle. When the story reached King Charles at Oxford that the battle was being refought, by ghosts in the sky, he sent some army officers who had been at Edgehill to investigate. The legend has it that they saw the battle and even recognized some of their dead comrades. Other tales have been told about the sites of Naseby, Marston Moor and others. This seems to hark back to the ages-old belief that those who are not properly buried are left to haunt this world instead of passing on to the next one.

Something similar seems to be behind the experiences of a woman who, in 1950, was walking home to the village of Letham in Angus in Scotland. She was a kilometre or so from the village when an apparition took form round her, continuing for a good twelve minutes, until she reached her home. There were moving torches in the distance up ahead. As she got closer, she saw dim figures searching the ground. Men were pulling up bodies, turning them over and scrutinizing each one. Later study of the history of the area revealed that the men had been dressed as ancient Picts. The whole place had once been a lake, and it was suggested that she had witnessed the soldiers turning over the bodies of their comrades looking for friends or relatives!

The same theories about spooks have been applied to battlefield ghosts. It's wishful thinking or the whistling of the wind or strange lights in the sky (such as the aurora borealis or luminescent clouds) that make people, already well versed in the bloody histories of such places, fantasize that they are seeing the battles re-enacted round them.

How one explains away a phantom bomber is harder. The ghost plane has been seen for more than thirty years, flying over the Derbyshire moors, near Hope. The last sighting was in May 1995. It was clearly in trouble, zooming low above an elderly fell walker, but it was absolutely silent and neither the sounds nor the debris of a crash were apparent. Research has revealed that two separate aircraft, a USAF Dakota and a Royal Canadian Air Force Lancaster, both crashed in the area during the Second World War, killing the entire crew on each occasion.

Casebook: The bowmen and the angels

Probably the most famous of all the tales of wartime ghosts is that of the Ghost Bowmen of Mons. The legend started at the end of 1914, when the German forces had pushed the British Expeditionary Force back through France. A story started going around of a miraculous event. At Mons, with the Germans just about to commit a devastating assault, ghostly images of St George and the bowmen of Agincourt imposed themselves between the opposing sides, allowing the British to slip away and retreat in safety.

It sounds like a legend – and it is. In September 1914, a story by Arthur Machen in the London *Evening Standard* called 'The Bowmen' had told just such a tale – a fictional one. When this explanation was reported, however,

The ghostly bowmen in action.

some soldiers wrote to say that, although it might have been a fictional story, such an event had happened, when a cloud of mysterious fog had appeared between the lines. The tales grew and changed, and then the cloud had become a host of glowing angels. By now people were wondering if Machen had been inspired by a real event – and the waters were far too muddied for anyone to make out the truth behind it all. These days it's regarded as nothing more than a legend that became a great piece of propaganda and raised people's morale during the dark days of the First World War.

FILE STATUS

Myth.

Ghostly recordings?

As you will discover as your investigations continue, it's easy enough to document what people see – or think they see. Actually explaining it is much harder, though there are plenty of theories to help.

From a totally sceptical perspective, it could be argued that no one sees ghosts as we normally define them: the undead remnants of someone's spirit. If (for whatever reason) they are not faking, people who see ghosts are either fooling themselves, are temporarily ill or are under the influence of something dubious, or they are crazy. This is certainly the line that the scientific establishment takes: ghosts don't exist; people are seeing optical illusions or hallucinations.

It's certainly true that most 'ghost' encounters can easily be explained by a bit of common sense. People do scare themselves and hear ghosts where there's nothing but a clanking radiator and some creaking floorboards. People do start to believe in phantoms so strongly that they start seeing grey-robed shapes out of the corner of their eye. Experts are becoming more confident that they can explain how and why people see things. Simple familiarity is often enough. In a paper for the *British Medical Journal* in 1971, Dr Robert Rees of mid-Wales reported that almost half the widowed people in his practice said they had experienced hallucinations of their dead spouses. They weren't frightened by them; rather, they were comforted.

Stone tapes and place memories

Set against all that, however, are the cases – like the Romans through the wall – that defy such dismissals. And it's from these that ghost investigators have derived an amazing but strangely plausible theory to explain Recording Ghosts.

Consider an ordinary cassette tape. That thin brown plastic tape is coated with nothing more than magnetized rust, but it can store sounds or even video pictures. The 'stone tape' theory suggests that certain elements are able to store images or emotions, and play them back at a later date, maybe again and again. Certain events – especially those stressful, traumatic times that generate an awful lot of emotional energy – somehow become imprinted within a location's stone walls. In the years or centuries that follow, nothing happens, but eventually the right conditions – such as the right combination of moisture, atmospheric pressure and electromagnetic energy – trigger off the recording.

It would certainly explain how some Recording Ghosts can be seen on several different occasions at the same location, and why some appear to be somewhat three-dimensional. It would explain how ghosts such as the York Romans can walk through walls; what Harry Martindale was seeing, perhaps, was just a sophisticated form of film playback or moving hologram.

So where's the proof, you ask. Well, scientists know that there are certain stones which can emit energy; quartz is especially good (you may have a watch powered by a small chip of it). However, there's still a long way to go before we get ghosts popping out of the walls all over the place. For starters, it would be helpful to discover the combination that allegedly triggers the image. Some people theorize that it requires an extra element: the chemical, emotional or even psychic suitability of the viewer him- or herself. It has long been suggested that certain people are more open to ghosts; but whether it is a natural or a supernatural power which allows such 'sensitives' to do so hasn't been determined.

Now all this is already way beyond what scientists can prove. To change this a little, to make it more believable, some suggested that it's only a mood that is transmitted. The rest, the theory goes, is then generated within the depths of the human mind. It's a fine compromise – it's a recording and a hallucination – but it's still nowhere near being proved.

On the other hand, who knows what will be discovered now that you are on the case?

It's Baaa–aaack!

Here's another myth that needs exploding. You'll become very familiar with this sort of story as you plough through all the inaccurate tripe that is written about ghosts. It's this sort of nonsense: 'Every 29th September, on the stroke of midnight, the headless White Lady, head tucked neatly under her arm, strolls through the Summer Room.'

Yeah, right. Since when?

The way ghosts are presented – and we're really talking about the way they are sold to tourists as entertainment now – one could almost draw up a diary. Almost every night one could be camped out in some crumbling ancestral pile or dingy cellar waiting for this or that ghost to appear, as expected. Your itinerary could run like this:

- 1st January, headless nun, Stoke Poges, midnight
- 2nd January, coach and horses, Dundee, midnight
- 3rd January, headless duck, Cheshire, midnight

and so on. You could perhaps even tick them off in your *Spook Spotter's Book of Spectres* as each one scared the living daylights out of you.

Such ghosts are termed 'anniversary ghosts', and the guidebooks which describe them will send you on a wild goose chase trying to see them – and failing. The theory is that ghosts always turn up to do a swift bit of haunting on the anniversary of their untimely death.

Dig a little deeper into such matters and you'll find some major inconsistencies. For a start, most of the ghosts which are alleged to turn up as regular as clockwork every year haven't actually been seen this century. Or if they have, it was at a totally different time and in a different place. If ghosts really did turn up that frequently and that reliably, do you not think that maybe just one or two people would hang around waiting for them, infra-red cameras, videos, EMU units and talcum powder at the ready?

Now, it's true that different people have seen the same ghost in the same location at various times. But that's a different matter; such sightings may be many decades apart. If you look at the way we measure time, further problems arise. For example, would your average ghost turn up on, say, the third Sunday of November, or would it show every 22nd November? And what would it do in a leap year? Older ghosts would have even more problems: in October 1752 we changed our calendar from the Julian to the Gregorian and lost eleven days in the process. Any ghost from before that date trying to keep an appointment is going to be eleven days early! Doh!

Unless that explains why the ghosts are never there when we turn up to see them ...

Way Back When

Recording Ghosts are hard enough to explain, but they are nothing compared to the phenomenon of the 'time-slip'. In these cases, witnesses don't just see a figure who once used to be alive – they see an entire scene, and they can walk through it. These are far rarer than Recording Ghosts but are not uncommon. Time-slips seem like a more sophisticated version of a Recording Ghost sighting. But are people observing a visual record which has been triggered, not just of a single figure but by an entire scene, complete with backgrounds, smells and all – or are they actually crossing into a different time-frame, albeit only for a moment?

One good example is the case, reported in *Fortean Times*, of two men who were using a metal detector late at night in a field near Telford, Shropshire, in October 1995. They had found several Roman coins and were continuing their search when they were startled by the sound of galloping horses. The noise came straight at them, causing the pair to run in separate directions! They did not see any horses, and the noises faded away. Investigating in the direction in which they had gone, the men came to a tall hedge which stretched across the middle of the field. When they came to the end of it at the side of the field, they turned around only to find that it had disappeared! They continued to search the now-empty field but could not find any footprints or any other clues. However, later researches revealed that the field was near the site of an old Roman garrison.

Such an encounter might still fall within the realm of the Recording Ghost. There are, however, some time-slips which are far more involving. From 1988 comes the case of a woman whom the accounts call 'Eleanor Ford'. She was on holiday in Burra, Australia, and one night she returned from having dinner with a friend, to find all the lights on in her rented cottage. Peering nervously in through the window, she saw a quite different room from the one she expected, and a woman in an old-fashioned dress sitting on a couch, talking to someone out of sight. Then the woman seemed to notice Ms Ford looking in through the window and she smiled. Ms Ford stepped back to make sure she was at the right cottage. Then she noticed that the curtains were as she had left them: drawn. She and her friend hurried inside but, once she got inside, the cottage was as she had left it.

So what was it she saw? If we accept that Recording Ghosts are replays of earlier scenes, it could perhaps have been a more sophisticated and elaborate recording. However, this does not tally with the idea that such 'ghosts' are initially imprinted by emotional trauma – for how could a building or a whole scene be so terrified or otherwise stressed that its emotional image is stored?

Others have suggested that, as the name implies, such encounters are nothing less than glimpses into another time or dimension. Whether these involve the viewer stepping back in time for a moment, or possibly the momentary transportation into the body or mind of someone present at the original scene, understanding it further requires the study of the way time itself works. One of the most common theories says – to simplify it massively – that time is a loop which is being reeled out slowly in front of us. If this is the case, the theory goes, we could perhaps be able to hop across the loop to another point in time and space. Alternatively, it could be that there are other dimensions, other worlds almost exactly like ours, that spin off from the world every single time someone makes a decision – perhaps time-slips are a brief glimpse into these? We'll stop there, because we need a lie-down.

Alternatively, it could just be that witnesses are mistaken.

Casebook: The Dieppe dredger

In August 1951 two women were on holiday in Puys, near Dieppe, France. Their second-floor room looked out over the beach where, in 1942, Allied troops had taken part in a disastrous raid. One night at 4.20 a.m. they were alarmed by extraordinary sounds that seemed to be coming from the beach. It was like 'a roar that ebbed and flowed', one said later. As it grew louder, they could hear guns, shellfire, aircraft dive-bombing and the cries of men. Over the following three hours they listened and made notes, terrified that they were somehow hearing the raid again.

The case was reported to the SPR, and many details of their story matched up with the times of different events during the raid. However, the file was eventually seen by an SPR member who had also holidayed in that part of France later the same month. He vividly remembered being woken up by a powerful dredger in the harbour that worked all night and made a noise 'like a zoo animal gone mad'. Further aspects of the affair weakened the case. The women had said that, although they had a guidebook on Dieppe, they claimed not to know any details. In fact, one of the women was identified as the wife of a wartime hero, and she herself had worked in Military Intelligence during the war. Furthermore, she had engaged in lengthy correspondence with the SPR on various matters concerning the paranormal. Finally, the guidebook they had taken with them had even mentioned how the Battle of Culloden was apparently being replayed in a ghostly fashion, years after the event!

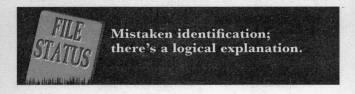

FILE STATUS

Mistaken identification; there's a logical explanation.

Casebook: An adventure

The most famous time-slip of all took place in 1901, again in France. A pair of women, the elderly Charlotte Moberley, Principal of St Hugh's College, Oxford, and Eleanor Jourdain, her younger Vice-Principal, were visiting the Palace of Versailles. After leaving the Galeries des Glaces, they decided to walk through the formal gardens to the Petit Trianon building much beloved of Marie-Antoinette. Not sure of the way, they took a path at random but, realizing they were lost, they stopped to ask the way of two men, gardeners by the look of the wheelbarrow and spade they had with them. More remarkable, though, were their long, grey-green coats and three-cornered hats. However, the men gave the ladies directions, in French, and they continued on their way. As they strolled along, both women began to feel strange, almost depressed, and the world seemed to take on an odd, two-dimensional feel. They heard the sound of footprints behind them, but nobody was there. An ugly man leered from a dark corner. Then a smiling man wearing a cloak and a sombrero gave them directions to the house.

As they neared it at last, Miss Moberley saw a woman, dressed in an old-fashioned costume and wearing a large white hat; she was sketching on the lawn, and she smiled as they passed. It was only much later that Miss Moberley discovered that her companion had not seen her – Marie-Antoinette, that is. When the pair arrived at the Petit Trianon, the atmosphere of unreality and gloom lifted again.

They kept the story to themselves, but nine years later their book, *An Adventure*, told the whole story. So had they stepped back in time and observed buildings and people dating from just before the French Revolution? It's hard to argue with it – until one takes a closer look, as recent ghost investigators have now done. For a start, the women did not write up their accounts until three months after the event, and the story was not finalized for nine years. Each woman wrote her own account, and there are many differences between them. It was a warm day for an elderly pair to be out walking; if they had drunk some wine at lunchtime, their perceptions could have been quite different. Some bright spark discovered that at the time Comte Robert de Montesquieu, obsessed with the eighteenth century, used to hold costume parties in the grounds. Another found details of a woman who would dress up as Marie-Antoinette and sit by the Petit Trianon to amuse tourists.

On the other hand, some of the buildings that the women were convinced they saw on their strange walk are no longer there, and to follow the paths they said they took would have required them – in 1901 – to have climbed over several brick walls. The case remains unexplained; you'll have to make up your own mind.

FILE STATUS

Unexplained.

But When the Film was Developed . . .

People continue to swear by the old saying, 'The camera never lies' – which is rather peculiar because, ever since photography was invented, it seems the camera has done little but lie! Photos are no guarantee of the truth. Double exposures, faults, long exposures, retouching, collage – all these tricks have been behind photographs which have claimed to show the 'truth' about ghosts. And still, despite all the many photos of alleged ghostly apparitions, not one has yet proved conclusively the existence of a supernatural being.

In the last twenty years there have been far fewer 'genuine ghost photos'. This is not because people are not producing photos of strange, ethereal beings. It's because we are more sophisticated; we are well versed in the tricks of films and television, and we've seen enough double exposures and blurred thumbs over the lens to spot a mistake when we see it.

Back in the middle of the last century, people were visually far less literate. Cameras were a novelty; with their miraculous snapping of images and chemical solutions they must have seemed like medieval alchemy to most people. We know that at the turn of the century, when the first cinema films were made and shown, people in the audience tried to run away from a sequence showing a speeding train; sixty years earlier, still photographs must have seemed just as astonishing. Few people had enough technical expertise or possessed a camera of their own, in order to question the photos of other people. And as result, some unscrupulous photographers exploited such ignorance for all they were worth. For if the camera is lying, it's a fair bet that the photographer is, too.

In the 1860s, around Boston in the USA, people went to William Mumler to have their photograph taken with a loved one. In this case, however, the loved one was likely to be dead, and would appear in the photo as a ghostly image hovering somewhere over the person's shoulder. Mumler had been attempting to take a self-portrait when he discovered how easy it was to take a double exposure. After all, in those days photographs used chemically treated plates; you opened the shutter and the image was imprinted – open it twice on two different scenes and you got a double exposure. Mumler went into business as a spirit capturer. He was fêted by the rich and famous, for his services did not come cheap. The patronage of

Abraham Lincoln's widow gave him much-needed credibility. Mumler said of the famous photo of her sitting with her husband looming above her that she had turned up with a veil covering her face, and that he had only recognized her when Lincoln's face turned up as the photo was developed. Strangely, however, the photograph shows Mrs Lincoln's face clearly. Oops. Eventually Mumler was exposed as a fraud, but over the years his tricks have inspired many other fakers.

These days we are far more sophisticated. We can watch films of approaching trains without jumping out of their way, nor do we believe that real dinosaurs are back and are stalking the earth. We are also more suspicious. It isn't enough for a photographer merely to plonk down a photo showing some fuzzy white shimmer; the story has to back it up. That's why so many modern ghost photos come complete with the line 'It wasn't until I had the photograph developed …' In other words, people think that if they claim to have been photographing a ghost in the first place, the world would be very dubious. On the other hand, saying that a weird image turned up totally by accident is rarely convincing either – does it mean that there really was nothing to see, or that the photographer was so lackadaisical that he did not notice what he was photographing? And why was he taking a photograph of a dusty staircase anyway? There is also a suggestion that if, as some believe, ghosts are manifestations of emotions, there shouldn't be any photographs of them at all – we can't take pictures of radio waves.

Young Greg Maxwell's 'Nanna' – or the photographer's thumb?

Most alleged ghost photographs have simple explanations; it seems only wishful thinking or some odd circumstance that even allows the possibility of there being something more to the case. For example, consider the photograph of thirty-month-old Greg Maxwell, from 1991. He's gazing at a white mist which appears to be hovering beside him. One's first instinct is to say, 'Oh, the photographer had her thumb in the picture.' But the background story throws doubt on that. About twelve months before the picture was taken, young Greg started saying, 'Old Nanna's here,' on odd occasions. It was his name for his great-grandmother, who had just passed on. Now the family think that this picture proves that Greg is seeing her ghost. Certainly his eyes seem to be looking at something. If nothing else, it's a lovely coincidence.

It is coincidence, too, that allows double exposures to be claimed as real. People argue that the odds against a double exposure producing a perfect image of a ghost standing in exactly the right place must be astronomical. They are – but consider how many millions of photos are snapped by people every year. Even the highest odds will produce a few perfect matches. Furthermore, there have also been rare cases when people have bought films that were already used, although they came in sealed boxes.

These days, video camcorders are far more popular than ever before, and there has been a rash of allegedly ghostly images produced. We heard of a wedding video that apparently showed the late father of the bride standing watching the happy proceedings from the shadows. This sort of ghostly image will occur more frequently as camcorder ownership spreads – but it will still prove very hard for a photographer just to slap down a convincing snap of a ghost, especially if he uses the words, 'But when the film was developed …'

Casebook: The Brown Lady

Raynham Hall in Norfolk has been home to Lord Townsend and his family for many generations. It is a very old house and has a reputation for being haunted. The most commonly seen ghost is that of a mysterious

Captain Provand's famous picture of the Brown Lady.

Brown Lady; she was first seen in 1835 and has been encountered many times since, including a strong sighting in 1960, often on the grand main staircase.

In September 1936 two photographers were snapping the house for a piece in *Country Life* magazine. At four in the afternoon, having already captured a number of outdoor and indoor locations, they were preparing to photograph the grand staircase when one of the pair, Indre Shira, appeared to see what he later described as an 'ethereal veiled form' moving down the stairs. He cried to his partner, Captain Provand, to take a picture immediately, which he apparently did. The Captain had not seen anything and he teased his assistant, saying ghosts were impossible. They took several more photos that afternoon, then headed for home. When the film was developed, it seemed that a semi-transparent, distinctly ethereal figure had indeed been captured.

So are we seeing a ghost or is our mind just jumping to conclusions? A sceptic would look at it and see little more than a foggy swirl. It looks more like a smear of grease or gel on the lens, or perhaps someone ran a finger down a semi-developed plate. Perhaps the other photographer did it to tease his gullible fellow. The emphasis on Shira's 'ethereal veiled form' seems to go against what we know about ghosts, which are usually far more solid. It seems more like a cliché than a genuine sighting. On the other hand, the house does have a history – though this fact could have convinced a gullible person even further. Whatever the truth, it's a fascinating photograph.

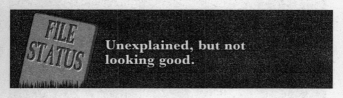

FILE STATUS

Unexplained, but not looking good.

Casebook: Photographing fairies

Of all the many old photographs of supernatural phenomena, none caused so much controversy as those taken by two young Yorkshire girls earlier this century. The most surprising thing about the case of the Cottingley Fairies, however, is that the file was allowed to remain open for so long. If you had been on the case, we have no doubt it would have been solved in an instant!

In 1917, ten-year-old Frances Griffiths and her mother were staying with Frances's older cousin, Elsie Wright, in Cottingley, Yorkshire. At the bottom of the Wrights' garden was a small strip of land, Cottingley Glen, an overgrown piece of woodland with a small stream and a waterfall. Frances and Elsie believed in fairies, and they had often drawn them and told stories about them. Both girls spent a considerable amount of time playing down in

But of course they're real fairies . . . The first (retouched) photograph.

the glen, and their parents were worried, not least by the muddy state of their clothes when they returned. Under pressure, Frances admitted they were going to watch the fairies; when pressed, Elsie backed up her cousin. The parents laughed and made fun of the girls over a number of weeks.

In July, the girls decided to take some photographs to 'prove' to the adults what they had seen. Arthur Wright had a camera and, after some persuading, he lent it to the girls so that Elsie could take a picture of Frances in the glen 'as a souvenir of her stay'. Arthur then developed the picture – to reveal a line of fairies dancing in front of Frances! He thought they were cardboard cut-outs; after all, Elsie had seen fairies for years. The girls, however, insisted that the picture was genuine, and took another.

Two years later, the two girls' mothers mentioned the photographs to a lecturer giving a talk on fairies and other folklore. Edward Gardner borrowed the snaps and had them cleaned up and sharpened. When he saw the new pictures, a local professional photographer, a Mr H.

Snelling, pronounced them totally genuine. They were
not double exposures, the pictures were not cut-outs and
there was no retouching, he insisted. Word began to
spread about the miraculous pair of pictures until it
reached the ears of Sir Arthur Conan Doyle, respected
author and creator of Sherlock Holmes. In the December
1920 issue of *Strand Magazine*, Doyle's report appeared
under the headline: FAIRIES PHOTOGRAPHED. AN EPOCH-
MAKING EVENT DESCRIBED BY A. CONAN DOYLE. A second article appeared in March 1921, then in 1922 a book,
The Coming of the Fairies, continued the revelations; by now
any doubts Doyle may have had were gone. Other so-
called experts also praised the photographs as genuine.
Meanwhile, sceptics produced their own fake fairy pictures; one even showed a ring of little elves frolicking in
front of a grumpy-looking Conan Doyle. The girls produced three more photographs and stuck doggedly to
their story – as they continued to do whenever the story
resurfaced over the decades.

What is remarkable about the whole case is how anyone could have believed in the pictures for an instant. The
fairies are so flat they look as if they have been cut out of
cardboard. They also have period hairdos and dresses.
But the girls insisted, and the experts backed them up.
After all, how could two young girls produce such clear,
obviously unfaked photographs, they argued. That is,
until one looks at the original negatives. Before they were
retouched and sharpened by Mr Gardner, the original
negatives show very blurry, flat scenes, not the crystal-
clear fairy photographs about which the world had mar-
velled.

Finally, in 1977, researcher Fred Getting stumbled
across an illustration in *Princess Mary's Gift Book* which
showed three dancing fairies in postures that were identical to those in the first photograph. By a neat coincidence,
the 1915 book had a piece in it by Arthur Conan Doyle.

At last, in 1981, Elsie and Frances came clean. Of
course they had been fakes, held up by hat-pins in the
long grass. The girls had been quite astonished that so
many adults had been convinced by their efforts: as Elsie

said in 1986, 'The joke was meant to last two hours. It has lasted seventy years.' To the end, although Elsie begged to differ, Frances still insisted that she really had seen fairies in Cottingley Glen and had just tried to show what they had looked like. Who knows, perhaps she did see fairies; she wouldn't be the first ten-year-old girl to do so.

FILE STATUS

Fakes that got very out of hand.

Haunting Ghosts

It is a strange fact, but the real, full-tilt, all-flags-flying, walking, clanking and moaning ghost encounters are the rarest of all the forms you will investigate. A sceptic might say that this is because it is very hard to support the tale of an encounter in which so many things happen. A believer in the Recording Ghost theories might counter this by saying that fully interactive ghosts are just very rare, requiring a very unusual set of circumstances to produce them. Others point out that the behaviour of Haunting Ghosts means that they cannot be explained by such theories, and that something else is going on. As you may deduce, there is no consensus of opinion on any of this, and no solid proof of anything at all!

Hauntings are a step forward from Recording Ghosts in that, although the images, sounds and whatever are similar, the ghosts seem to respond to events round them with a purpose and sometimes an intelligence. Unlike the time-slip situation, however, they are firmly based in the here and now. There is some debate that such ghosts are visible versions of poltergeists. However, there are some differences, not least in their behaviour. Poltergeists, as we shall see later, are mischievous spirits; Haunting Ghosts often appear to have a more subtle purpose. Some want to comfort the bereaved or pass on messages, it seems; others want to deliver a curse!

Haunted houses

Sad to say, tracking down a genuine haunting will prove to be a real problem. Oh yes, there are plenty that are reported. Sometimes it seems as if every third building in every last street is home to some form of paranormal activity, and of course every mansion hall or public house more than twenty years old wouldn't be complete without its resident phantom. Because Haunting Ghosts fulfil so many of the clichés about ghosts, most of the cases in the files are little more than glorified folk-tales, which makes them useless for the purposes of serious study, no matter how entertaining they may be. The idea of the haunted house is so widespread that it's hard to shake off.

However, we know from the files that ghosts don't just turn up in ancient manor houses or ancestral seats. Indeed, if a ghost is reported in such a location, it is far more likely that one can write it off as nothing more than a family tale. The Radiant Boy, for example, is said to haunt the Lytton family of Knebworth House, Hertfordshire. His most celebrated manifestation was in 1820, when he appeared to Lord Castlereagh, who later committed suicide. The ghost is said to look like a naked child of about eleven with a bright, fresh face. Castlereagh said before his death that the vision emerged from a fireplace in a bedroom. Take a look at that date again: over 175 years ago – far too long for serious study.

Some people positively encourage the myth of a ghost attached to their stately home; these days a hall isn't properly 'historical' unless it has its fair share of spectres and spooks which bring in the tourists and may even add a side-line in Ghostwatching evenings. Other benefits can arise too: in 1993, Boy's Hall at Willesborough, Kent, was put on the market, its chief feature being that it was guaranteed haunted. The Jacobean mansion had been the scene of many grisly events and was said to be stalked by the ghostly figure of a woman. As part of the Property

Misdirection Act, estate agents must inform potential buyers of all hazards associated with a property, so they had little option but to mention it. The hall sold, by the way.

It isn't just the grand old mansions which give homes to ghosts these days, far from it. Apparitions are reported everywhere, from libraries and churches to modern blocks of flats. Pubs are a popular location for a haunting. The Ilchester Arms, near Yeovil in Somerset, was the scene of a recent encounter. Repeated sounds were heard: heavy barrels being rolled across cobbles which no longer exist, and the sound, every evening, of someone typing; more annoyingly, glasses would disappear, only to reappear two days later. A local sensitive, Flo Essex, visited the pub and declared that the ghost was that of Tizzy, a mischievous teenage girl.

The source of many tales concerning haunted pubs must again be put down to their age and a bit of story-telling. This is still going on. In the village of Sandhutton, near Thirsk in Yorkshire, you will find the Busby Stoop pub. Until sixteen years ago the landlord kept under lock and key an old oak chair that was said to have been the one in which a murderer called Busby sat and had his last earthly pint before being hanged in 1702. As he was being dragged out to the scaffold, they say he cursed the crowd and said that anyone who sat in the chair would die. Over the years, various deaths have been attributed to the chair in all seriousness. But it's not true. The chair and its legend were introduced in the late 1940s by the pub's landlord, Tom Collins, presumably to make the place a tourist attraction. Nowadays the chair sits harmlessly in the Thirsk Museum.

You will find stories of hauntings in some surprising locations. We have heard of several haunted banks, for example. The most famous is Coutts and Co., the Queen's own bank, whose branch in the Strand, London, was haunted by a headless black figure in 1992. Still in London, just about every theatre has its own resident phantom or three. The Theatre Royal, Drury Lane, for example, has its Man in Grey, a figure dressed in early eighteenth-century riding clothes, a wig and a three-cornered hat, who is seen wandering the Upper Circle. On the other hand, theatre folk are a superstitious lot at the best of times, with their pre-performance superstitions about 'breaking a leg' and not naming 'the Scottish play'.

Ghost on the highway

But hauntings aren't just found indoors. Many areas of moorland, wooded hilltops, lakes and standing stones have their own resident ghost. Several haunted caves are on file, though such reports may be retellings of old myths about goblins and elves. Mines, however, are very often said to be haunted; this is understandable when one considers the dangerous location – few mines would be without their grisly tally of fatalities.

People have also made strong claims for roads being haunted. Among the best-researched is Blue Bell Hill, the highest point of the North Downs, near Maidstone in Kent, which has been the scene of multiple sightings of a ghostly girl. In November 1992, at around midnight, a motorist had just reached the crossroads at the foot of the hill when a young girl stepped out in front of his car. Thinking he had hit her, he screeched to a halt – but there was no one there. His car showed no marks of any

The road over Blue Bell Hill, Kent. Scary.

collision. When he turned up at Maidstone Police Station, white-faced and shaking, the police sat him down and told him about the legends associated with the place. Another driver reported the same occurrence two weeks later. Researchers have pointed to a car-crash one November evening in the early 1970s in which a young woman from Rochester was killed the day before she was due to be a bridesmaid. The recurring November sightings remind one of a Recording Ghost, but this apparition seems to have a mind of its own.

Similar stories are found in many parts of the world. Some drivers have reported seeing a phantom coach and horses, or a ghostly highwayman galloping amidst the traffic. There are also reports that roads are 'jinxed' due to the number of crashes that take place on them; perhaps over time the story will change and the blame will be put on one specific ghost.

The vanishing hitchhiker myth

We have mentioned urban myths several times already. These powerful pieces of folklore are passed on from person to person as if they were true stories. These days, of course, experts are on the case and can instantly point out when such tales are just variations on an older story. Among the most famous is that of The Vanishing Hitchhiker. Here's the basic version:

A friend of a friend and his wife were driving along a country road late one night. Up ahead they saw a young woman hitchhiking, and so they stopped to give her a lift. She hopped into the back seat and told them that she lived in a recognizable house fifteen minutes down the road, but after that she was silent and just looked out of the window. When the couple arrived at the house she had described, they turned around to say they had arrived – but she was gone! Thinking this was odd, they went and knocked at the door. The woman who answered told them that she used to have a daughter as they described, but that she had disappeared five years ago. Today would have been her birthday. Woooh!

You'll come across similar stories during your investigations. The details will be modified to fit your part of the world, a popular make of car and so on, but the theme will be the same. Experts have collected versions of that one with horses, carriages and motorbikes, from the farthest corners of America, Eastern Europe and Australia. Watch out for urban myths; they are always too good to be true.

Drive me crazy

As well as haunted roads, there are literally hundreds of stories about vehicles which have become home to a ghostly spirit. In the early 1980s, John Homer, of Worthing, West Sussex, had a sporty green Vauxhall Cavalier. Sometimes when he was driving it, it felt as if someone behind him was pushing their knee into the back of the seat. Occasionally he would 'hear' a voice in his head warning him of an upcoming hazard. In his rear-view mirror he kept seeing a red car that would disappear if he pulled over to let it pass. He had several accidents, all of which involved the car's left-side front wing being dented. One day he felt a genuine presence in the back seat, and out of the corner of his eye he thought he saw in the mirror a middle-aged woman. In the end, he sold the car – it was last seen on a repair truck, its left front wing all smashed in!

Ghosts who haunt motorbikes have also been reported. In one incident, a woman was watching her husband repair a motorbike he had bought when a young man walked into the yard and also stood watching. She asked her husband to introduce her but the man had vanished. When she described him to her husband, he told her it sounded like the previous owner of the motorbike, who had died two years previously.

Even if we have no specific evidence for a ghost, people will often attribute the poor performance of a vehicle to a 'jinx'. During the Second World War, pilots would talk of their aircraft having 'gremlins', and the word soon came to mean a mischievous little goblin which breaks engines (you know the films, we're sure).

James Dean, the teen-idol actor, was killed in 1955 when his Porsche crashed. After that, the car seemed to be jinxed. Bought by a garage owner, it slipped while being unloaded and broke a mechanic's leg. Its engine was sold to a doctor who was killed when his new car crashed in a race. Another car received the drive shaft; it spun out of control and the driver was injured. A racing driver who bought two tyres was almost killed when both exploded simultaneously. The smashed and dented car body was sent round America as part of a road safety exhibition. In Sacramento it fell off its mounting and broke a teenager's hip. Later, the truck carrying it was in an accident – the driver was thrown out and killed when the car rolled off the back on to him; in Oregon, the same truck slipped its hand-brake and rolled into a shop. In New Orleans, finally, the car fell into eleven different pieces while mounted on the display. Now that's a jinx!

Planes, too, have their fair share of gremlins. In one classic case, however, two ghosts seem to have made it their business to fight back against them. In December 1972, Eastern Airlines Flight 401, a Lockheed L-1011 Tri-Star, crashed in the Florida Everglades, killing over a hundred passengers. The plane's auto-pilot had a fault: it turned off if the steering column was pushed a certain way. Thereafter, ghosts of the Captain, Bob Loft, and Second Officer Don Repo were supposedly seen on many other Tri-Stars; sometimes they warned staff of potential hazards, on other occasions Repo was seen fixing bits of equipment before vanishing. Official reports were vague in their findings, but it was certain that many trained personnel were experiencing something very peculiar!

Nowadays, as machines become more sophisticated but we understand them more clearly, there seem to be fewer reports of hauntings. However, we did hear shadowy reports of a computer in Cheshire, in December 1984, which started giving out strange messages that purported to come from the ghost of Thomas Harden. The messages appeared on every one of twelve different computers the witness tried, and linguists seemed convinced that Harden's ghost was using authentic sixteenth-century English. Sadly we have no further details.

These days, there is an organization in New York that does nothing but log tales of haunted computers. With the rise of the Internet there are already some on-line urban myths about ghosts of the World Wide Web and the like; eventually, no doubt, these will manifest themselves as full-scale ghost sightings.

Ghosts ahoy!

Sailors are a superstitious lot. It's probably because they spend half their voyages sitting on deck splicing mainbraces or knitting sails while waiting for something more interesting to happen. It's no wonder their minds begin to wander round about the time they have to yell, 'Six bells and all's well!'

Probably the most famous myth about a haunted ship concerns the *Flying Dutchman*. This legendary vessel, a bringer of bad luck to all who see her, inspired not only Coleridge's *Rime of the Ancient Mariner* but also a stage show in London in the 1820s and Wagner's opera of 1843. The latter's version of the story tells of a Dutch captain, Vanderdecken, who has sworn an oath to round the Cape of Good Hope even if it takes an eternity, and who sails there still. One famous real-life sighting was reported in the journal of the teenage princes, George (later King George V) and Albert Victor, who were sailing round the world in 1881. However, they did not see the boat themselves, and one has to wonder whether they were having their legs pulled by the sailors. Other reports, however, have come in over the years. A ship on convoy in the Polynesian Islands during the Second World War saw a large sailing vessel, moving without using her sails and which was invisible to radar. Lit up as if by floodlights on her deck, she hung around for a few minutes before slipping very quickly behind them and fading away.

Slightly more credence has been given to the story of the liner, the *Great Eastern*. This ship, which seemed jinxed from the moment she was launched, was involved in all sorts of collisions, and she was always prey, her crew said, to the sound of ghostly knocking. Eventually, investigation revealed the skeleton of a hapless riveter, accidentally entombed alive between the iron walls of the vessel's double hull during her construction. Or so the legend has it; i.e., the story is probably just another myth.

One case which was investigated far more rigorously concerned the liner *Queen Elizabeth 2*. In 1974, while crossing the Atlantic, Radio Officer Alan Holmes received the signal 'GKS GBTT QSX AREA 1A'. It was a standard position check, but using a code that was years out of date. When he eventually managed to translate it, he discovered that it had come from the old liner the *Queen Mary* – which had been pensioned off in 1967! While it has been known for radio signals to bounce off the moon and be picked up in Australia, this one seemed to have been flying around for years. Perhaps a bored radio officer on another boat was playing a joke.

We should perhaps point out that, despite all the legends of the *Flying Dutchman*, the *Marie Celeste* and the like, there are genuine cases of ghost ships. *Fortean Times* reported the curious case of the *Baychimo*, a cargo-steamer registered in London and owned by the Hudson's Bay Company. This vessel was abandoned in 1931 after being trapped in the ice north of Canada. During the next few years she was rediscovered and boarded several times, both when trapped in the ice-floes and floating free, but it has never been possible to sail her back to a port. The vessel was last sighted in 1962, more than three decades after first being abandoned. Who knows, perhaps she is out there still …

A ghostly menagerie

In the files there are plentiful reports of animal ghosts. This isn't so unusual – after all, we spend much of our lives in the company of pets or livestock. Cats and dogs are the most commonly reported ghostly animals, and this is only to be expected: as well as being among our most common pets, they are often also the ones to which we are closest. Just as a widow may see the familiar image of a dead spouse, so many people think they can still see their beloved mutt or moggy after they have passed away.

There are, however, plenty of tales of more extraordinary creatures in the annals of ghost investigators. In 1816, for example, a sentry at the Tower of London was startled by an enormous bear! He lunged at it in panic, but his weapon passed straight through and he fainted dead away. When he awoke, the creature had gone. Historians know that bears were kept at the Tower back in the thirteenth century.

A little more commonplace is the story of the ghost which left a peculiar sticky gloop all over the furniture in a house in Leicester at the end of 1991. A vicar who called in to assist the haunted family seemed to see the figure of a woman – and also that of a young goat, which was, ahem, spraying stuff everywhere.

In the files of the Society for Psychical Research there is the case from 1908 of the phantom pig of Newbury, Berkshire. The giant white porker with an unusually long snout was reported walking behind people in the village. As the SPR delved deeper, they heard further tales about ghostly donkeys, cows and other farm animals. Eventually the animals seemed to be traced back to a farm that had failed; the farmer had killed himself and left the poor creatures to starve. Ah!

There are reports of ghostly farm animals from many rural parts of the country; and one might expect, if one were to look into reports in, say, Egypt, that one would find similar cases of ghostly camels or oxen, for example. But if you really want weird, try to find out more about the headless duck of Cheshire. We have few details, but reportedly this phantom fowl used to haunt a lane between Stoak and Stanney in the last century! Which begs the question, did it emit an unearthly quack – and, if so, how?

Larger birds have come to have more mythical meanings. Many are seen as portents of doom or signs of change. White swans traditionally foretell the death of a bishop of Salisbury, for example. Similarly, the Oxenham family of Devon were, so legend has it, haunted for generations by a heron whose appearance heralded an imminent death in the family.

Black dogs

We are now firmly in the land of legend and folk-tales, so while we're here let's pause to consider one of the commonest types of ghostly animal. Black dogs have been seen in all parts of the British Isles for centuries. OK, so sometimes they are white, grey, brown or tan-coloured. One thing is for sure: they are all enormous, have very shaggy coats and their saucer-sized eyes blaze with supernatural fire!

In East Anglia, where one was last seen in 1989, it is called Black Shuck (possibly derived from the Anglo-Saxon *scucca*, demon or devil), in Lancashire Trash or Skriker, in Dorset the Tow Dog, on the Isle of Man the Mauthe Doog or Moddey Dhoo. On Dartmoor, in Devon, it is the Wish Hound of Wistman's Wood and was the inspiration for Conan Doyle's *The Hound of the Baskervilles*.

Possibly the most famous of them all is the Black Dog of Bungay, in Suffolk. At the height of a raging thunderstorm, in August 1577, the ravening beast burst into a church in the village and went on the rampage, killing two people. Later at Blytheborough it injured several more, and left its burnt black claw-marks in the church door – where they can still be seen! Some researchers have

How the Black Dog of Bungay hit the headlines in 1577.

identified this case as a strike of ball-lightning; but it was all too long ago to pin down now, worse luck.

Black dogs are mythical creatures that belong firmly in the realm of folk-tales. These days, of course, people are happier seeing large wild cats all over the place, but we're sure there is no relation between the two phenomena – is there?

Seeing things

Many of the cases we have looked at have their basis in folk-tales, but there are always incidents where more is going on than even a keen investigator like yourself will realize initially. Pushed to offer an explanation for a full haunting, what would you say? Follow our handy break-down of explanations; it runs from the most likely to the furthest out.

Fake or mistake: Look at your witnesses. If they are in their nineties, half deaf and are wearing milk-bottle specs, the odds of them making an accurate sighting are minimal. Similarly, if a person is already a 'believer' and is talking of having definitely, unquestionably seen a ghost, be wary; this person may even have some idea as to the ghost's identity. As we've already discussed under Recording Ghosts, it's often the case that witnesses look in the history books to see who it was they would have seen. Flip back far enough, and one's bound to find a monk, nun, heartbroken noblewoman or fifteenth-century mur-derer who will fit the bill.

Stories, we know only too well, grow in the telling. In some cases this is understandable, as with the Cottingley Fairies, where events just get out of hand. Others get passed on by word of mouth, and details always change via 'Chinese whispers'. People happily tell 'true stories' they know to be fake. It's when people start taking them seriously that problems arise.

A question of suggestion: As we've already noted, old central heating and creaking floorboards are far more common than ghosts. The strange lights on your ceiling are really just cars going by; that scrabbling in the eaves is just a pigeon on the roof – usually. But people continue to delude themselves, either quite unconsciously or semi-deliberately. When Anglia Television showed a documentary about a ghost hunter staking out Morley Old Hall in Norfolk in 1964, a dozen people rang in to say they'd seen a ghost on the show. It turned out they had mistaken a damp patch on an old wall in the background for a shadowy hooded figure!

Our unconscious mind stores far more than we realize. When, on the rare occasions we remember our dreams, we are sometimes startled by what our mind has stored away and then played back. Suggestions that somehow spirits are sending us telepathic messages – 'for how else could I have known that?' – will so often turn out to be merely a properly working subconscious.

Suggestions are more dangerous when several people are involved. The phenomenon of 'mass hysteria' arises because people trigger one another off, apparently giving credibility and support to outlandish suggestions. Panics start and cases spiral out of control, even though the panic may all be based upon shaky ground.

Hallucination generation: Some people really do just 'see things'. These can be caused naturally or through medical conditions or by accident. For example, Vicki Branden was terrified by a ghostly biker while walking her dog in 1974. Upon returning to her car she found that a can of de-icing spray had been leaking and had filled the vehicle with fumes – and it was this that had caused her to hallucinate.

Many ghosts are seen 'just as I was dropping off …'. A 'hypnagogic' vision occurs when our subconscious kicks in as we fall asleep; it may cause us to think we have seen a ghostly figure. Even more likely, similar 'hypnopompic' visions occur on the point of waking; they are often continuations of a dream.

Lucid dreams are those which seem so real that the dreamer thinks he or she is genuinely awake. On rare occasions these may be *onion-skin dreams*, in which a person dreams he or she wakes up and starts the routine of the day – only then to wake up properly.

More serious are medical conditions such as *temporal lobe epilepsy*. Sufferers have talked about seeing and hearing ghosts during seizures, complete with creaky floors and all the familiar trappings. Such conditions are caused by glitches when the two sides of the brain try to communicate. Most healthy people also experience very mild versions of the same problem, if very rarely.

Are you receiving?: As with Recording Ghosts, perhaps the visions are generated by trapped emotional resonances, which are then blown up by our brains into full-scale encounters. This may also correspond with Crisis Apparitions. Perhaps only 'sensitives' can pick up and interpret such signals, though they may be bouncing around for everyone to see, if only we could. Such theories, which rely on a form of ESP or telepathy, are beyond proof at present, despite decades of research. If such visions are created by telepathy, it would have to be directed at more than a single receiving mind, for how else would several people see the same ghost?

Mine's a double: More fanciful are the theories about the 'etheric double'. This stems, at least in part, from ancient beliefs in astral planes and witchcraft, and introduces serious doubts into a supposedly scientific theory. Everything that exists, the theory says, has a non-physical counterpart that exists in 'psychic space'. This realm of psychic energy sometimes intersects normal, physical space, allowing us to see and interact with it. Erk!

So strong is some researchers' belief that there must be a life after death, in one form or another, that they have proposed the existence of particles they have called psychons, which are to psychic space what atoms are to the real world. The problem is that such theories are being considered to explain something for which there is precious little evidence except for reported ghost sightings. Several investigators have, near the ends of their lives, entered into pacts with friends, promising to return and find some way of getting in touch if there genuinely is life after death. When he passed away in 1979, researcher J. Gaither Pratt left behind a closed combination lock and promised to communicate the combination from 'the other side'. The lock has never been opened.

So many theories, so little proof. As you continue your investigations, keep your wits about you. Who knows, you may pick up the vital piece of evidence that will crack these problems once and for all. While you are solving the mystery of the age, ponder on this one: if ghosts really are the spirits of the dead, why do they appear to be wearing clothes?

Casebook: Borley Rectory

Harry Price checking his facts.

The most famous ghost investigator of all time was a man called Harry Price. Up until his death in 1948, he had been investigating Britain's most perplexing cases for thirty years. During his lifetime, his greatest case was that of 'the most haunted house in England' – the affair of

Borley Rectory. However, the case is also a tremendous demonstration of how reputation and rumour are upset by the cold, hard facts.

Harry Price began his career with a youthful interest in stage magicians and hypnotists; as an amateur conjurer he was apparently fairly skilled, though he never performed on stage. Instead, like Harry Houdini in the USA, he used his interest to expose fraudulent mediums who used sleight-of-hand and other trickery to dupe people into thinking they were talking to a ghost. After some success, in 1926 he opened the National Laboratory for Psychical Research; four years later, his exposure of the fraudulent Austrian medium Rudi Schneider made him famous. In the resulting flap, what he discovered was disputed and criticized, but Price was unstoppable.

His philosophy was simple. Although he had access to what were at the time the latest advances in cameras, thermometers, stop-watches, microscopes and X-ray equipment, it was usually enough simply to be truly observant. If something strange happened while he was present, he'd simply seal the doors and windows with thread or adhesive tape and scatter powder on the floor.

In 1928 Harry Price first became involved with the case that was to occupy him for eleven strange years. Borley Rectory was a decrepit, rambling nineteenth-century house on the border between Essex and Suffolk, with a reputation for ghostly behaviour going back for years. It had been built in the 1860s by the Reverend H. Bull for his family and fourteen children; an extra wing and a cottage in the grounds were added in 1875. Legend had it that it stood on the site of an ancient monastery, and tales were told of a ghostly nun who, along with black shapes and a ghost coach, had apparently been seen many times around the turn of the century. These may have stemmed from the Reverend Bull himself, who was a notorious story-teller; certainly the legend of the monastery was just that – research has proved that there was nothing on the site of Borley Rectory.

In 1928, the new Rector, Eric Guy Smith, arrived to take up residence. He listened to all of the ghostly stories associated with his house and, although he had seen nothing himself, he was intrigued enough to write to the *Daily Mirror* asking for the address of a psychic researcher. First the *Mirror* sent down a staff reporter, who wrote up a story of headless horsemen and ghoulish nuns, the sound of dragging footsteps in empty rooms – much as one of today's tabloids would! Harry Price, taken on by the *Mirror*'s editor to look into the case properly, arrived some days later. He immediately noted that the place was in bad repair and rat-infested, but that the Reverend Smith refused to countenance the presence of ghosts. However, as soon as Price arrived, peculiar things started to happen: bells in the servants' quarters wouldn't stop ringing, stones were thrown by unseen hands, a vase smashed on its own and ghostly footsteps echoed through the house.

You will believe a brick can fly; Borley Rectory, 1944.

Sightseers, lured by the newspaper reports, turned up in droves. Eventually the rector and his wife moved out; in 1930, the new rector arrived from Canada, and then things really started to happen.

The new man was the elderly Reverend Lionel Foyster; he was accompanied by his young wife, Marianne. As soon as they moved in, barely a day or night went past without something odd happening. Ghostly writings turned up on the walls, addressed to Marianne but containing little more than her name and indecipherable scribbles. Small fires broke out spontaneously, keys jumped out of locks, small objects flew about and furniture was overturned. All manner of phantoms were seen, including a disembodied black hand, a little girl in white, the ghostly nun, the coach and horses and a headless man. Price and his team spent long periods at the Rectory investigating, but they could come up with few solutions and little to ease the problems. In 1935, after five crazy years, the Foysters gave up and moved out; in 1937, after the Rectory had stood, empty, for two years, Harry Price himself rented it. His team of ghost investigators studied the house intently, but in 1939 the house was destroyed by fire. A few years later the ruin was demolished and the foundations were torn up to leave no trace. Price wrote up his experiences in a pair of best-selling books, *The Most Haunted House in England* and *The End of Borley Rectory*, and he was proclaimed the greatest, most fearless, most thorough ghost hunter in the world.

Dubious evidence

At the time, some people were naturally sceptical of Harry Price. He was a showman, and his appetite for publicity made him enemies in the Society for Psychical Research, some of whose members thought he was bringing proper scientific study into disrepute. It is possible that some of their misgivings were well founded. Since Price's death there has been a flood of contradictory evidence which seems to cast doubt on many of his findings.

The basic summary of the 1956 SPR report was that Price had got hold of a potentially good case and he had exploited it for all it was worth. He had deliberately obscured certain facts that would have enabled outside observers to determine whether apparently strange events were of normal or paranormal origin. He suppressed evidence that contradicted his theory that the house was haunted, and he may even have stooped to fraud on several occasions to provide good 'copy'.

When *Life* magazine published a picture of a brick flying through the air as Borley was being demolished, Price claimed in all seriousness that it might be the very first genuine photograph of an object being teleported by a poltergeist. The *Life* reporter begged to differ, and he wondered why Price had conveniently 'forgotten' that, when the picture was taken, several builders were at work behind the wall from which the brick had emerged. Others testified to Price's twisting of the evidence. A newspaperman had once been hit on the head by a stone while walking with him. When he grabbed the ghost hunter, he found the man's pockets were crammed with pebbles! Two members of the SPR walking with Price through the darkened rectory were startled by spooky sounds rather like the rustling of Cellophane – and later they noticed a roll of the stuff in Price's briefcase.

His investigation methods were called into question too. For example, none of Price's chosen team of investigators was an expert on the paranormal. Worse, he had instructed them all using his notorious handbook, the 'Blue Book', which made the fatal mistake of telling the investigators the sorts of ghostly phenomena they were likely to be facing – in other words, they were expecting to see ghosts before they even got there!

Further culprits

The SPR file examined all the reported phenomena and reached conclusions that were quite different from Price's. The footsteps and whisperings were due to an unusual acoustical effect which relayed sounds from the adjacent cottage into the house. Stories emerged of how the young Bull children would play tricks by operating an old water pump to make spooky sounds echo through the house. Keys may have 'jumped' from locks due to air pressure and draughts. The bells could have been triggered by mice and rats gnawing on the wires.

There was also plenty of scope for human hoaxing. The house could be entered by three doors or via a trapdoor in the courtyard which led to the cellar, and there were three separate staircases. The severest phenomena centred on young Mrs Foyster, who was known to hate the place and wanted to leave. In the reports, she is almost never present (or at least in sight) when the phenomena started. The Foysters' previous posting had been in Canada, just a short distance away from the site of the alleged Great Amherst Mystery, a famous poltergeist case exposed as trickery; she could certainly have been inspired by that case. When SPR investigators checked 103 different incidents of the bells ringing, 99 depended totally on her word alone that she hadn't caused them.

Interviewed in the late 1970s, Marianne Foyster allegedly claimed that her ageing husband had also been exaggerating the phenomena. He had been writing a mostly fake account of events in the hope of earning money so she would be provided for after his death. She also believed, however, that Price was not fooled by their hoaxes but ignored their deceptions so that he could publicize the case ever more widely.

Reputation was certainly important to Harry Price. He always claimed he was the son of a wealthy paper manufacturer from an old Shropshire family; his father was really an elderly London grocer and they lived in a run-down street in New Cross. His early writings on rare coins were found to be plagiarized copies of obscure pamphlets. Throughout his life he puffed up his background and reputation – not lying, perhaps, but exaggerating it far beyond the truth.

These days, three bungalows have been built where Borley Rectory once stood. The site is still a place of pilgrimage for many amateur ghost hunters. Over the years, people have claimed to have seen all kinds of spectres in the grounds, including the infamous spectral nun and the phantom coach and horses that started the whole affair off in the first place.

FILE STATUS

Too long ago, alas, to judge, but some events were definitely exaggerated or deliberately faked.

Making Ghosts

On Hallowe'en night in 1992, the BBC transmitted the infamous *Ghostwatch* programme. It was a spoof as-it-happens documentary, presented by Michael Parkinson, about a poltergeist infestation. It was totally fake but was presented as real, with unexpected cuts in power, film of strange lights and actors pretending to be terrified. Many viewers believed the show was true, however; some rang the BBC to say they'd experienced poltergeist phenomena during the programme.

It sounds like the start of one of those urban myths. Such tales do seem to explain far too many alleged ghosts for comfort. Martin Tupper's 1858 novel, *Stephen Langton*, told the tale of poor drowned Emma. She was allegedly bathing in the Silent Pool, near Guildford, Surrey, when King John passed by and spied her. When he waded in to grab her, she swam away but drowned in deep water. However, although she is one hundred per cent fictitious, she has been heard crying for help – and occasionally even seen splashing – in the pool!

From time to time, those who study urban myths make up plausible-sounding legends and see how far and wide they spread, and how quickly. Similar experiments have been tried with ghosts. In the 1980s, sceptical researcher Frank Smythe came up with the tale of a ghostly clergyman who haunted Ratcliffe Wharf in London's Docklands. He wrote the story up in a ghost magazine, then sat back to see what would happen. Over the next twelve months or so, other writers researching their own ghost books included the fake in their roster of tales. Then several witnesses reported seeing the ghost in the Docklands area! When Smythe told them it was pure invention, one refused to believe him, implying that the writer must have thought he made it up but had really picked up on the presence of a genuine spirit and created his story under its influence. Meanwhile, people still are reporting sightings of the shadowy figure of a vicar on Ratcliffe Wharf!

The case of 'Philip' was even more sophisticated. In Toronto, Canada, from 1972 onwards, a research group led by Dr A. Owen invented the ghost of a long-dead English nobleman. They made up a whole life-story for him, as detailed as a historical novel. He was a contemporary of Oliver Cromwell, they decided; he was married but fell in love with a gypsy girl. She had been burnt at the stake for witchcraft and he had killed himself. Ever since, they said, his ghost had been seen strolling along the battlements of his estate.

Then they held meetings for months and months, treating Philip as a real dead spirit and trying to contact him. Eventually, in late 1973, he turned up and replied to them, communicating details of his (resolutely made-up) life. After a year, the experts had difficulty controlling the experiment; Philip had become so real, he was behaving like a real ghost! At one point an exasperated investigator snapped and told Philip he didn't really exist, whereupon the spirit vanished; it took many months of effort to make the 'ghost' return.

As the researchers concluded, despite being a product of their own minds, something had animated this phantom. Had the unconscious mind of the group created a ghost entity and, if so, is this how all ghosts are made? Or did they just imagine the whole thing? Spooky!

One Knock for Yes

Some people have always claimed to be able to communicate with ghosts. Such 'mediums' have been recorded since primitive times. In the middle of the last century, perhaps in reaction to the expansion of science and technology, there was a huge growth in people who believed in communication with the spirits, for which mediums were a necessary go-between. However, the whole movement appears to have started with a fake, and it has been prone to hoaxes and swindles ever since.

In 1848, the Fox family were living in a small house in Hydesville, New York State. The house had a reputation for being haunted, with all sorts of creaks and bangs being heard. One night, while in bed, the two youngest daughters, Margaret and Kate, decided to try to talk to their ghost. They asked it to knock once for yes, twice for no – and they were amazed when 'something' did just that! They devised a more sophisticated code and began to have long conversations with the spirit. When the story got out, people flocked to the Fox sisters to see for themselves. Other people began to communicate with 'the spirits' using the same knocking methods. It was a sensation that blossomed so quickly that by 1852 an enormous convention of these 'Spiritualists' was held in Cleveland, Ohio. People with the gift, mediums, became an asset to one's social circle and were always a hit at parties.

The craze had got so out of hand, in fact, that when Margaret and Kate confessed in public in 1855 that they had made all the noises themselves by cracking their toe-joints, no one believed them. The women were forced to withdraw their confessions. In 1888, just before she died, Margaret demonstrated before a packed crowd how she did, indeed, fake it all.

By then, society had taken mediums to its heart. It was the time of William Mumler and his fake ghost photographs (see above); most mediums were similarly deceitful. Many stories have come down from that time of miraculous performances at which a medium, helped by the

This is not a fake. Honest. A French medium in action, 1890s.

spirits, would reveal intimate details of a person's life, fore-tell the future, produce small trinkets (called 'apports') from nowhere, make the furniture rock about and generally put on an astonishing show. They took advantage of people's willingness to believe in their 'powers'.

Luckily there were persistent investigators around at the time who soon saw through such tawdry conjuring tricks. Eusapia Paladino was in mid-session when two researchers, swathed in black clothing, crept under a 'miraculously' levitating table and found her lifting one of its legs up with her foot. In England, medium Helen Duncan was convicted of fraud when, after allegedly producing the spirit of a little girl along with the tell-tale sound of tearing fabric, the lights were flipped on and caught her hastily stuffing a newly torn vest inside her dress. Among the most zealous unmaskers of fraudulent mediums was the American conjurer and escapologist, Harry Houdini. He knew only too well how people did magic tricks – so he made it his life's work to expose people who claimed to be doing something paranormal. When he tied up a medium suspected of being able to slip her bonds and move about a room causing strange noises – surprise, surprise! – the spirits that day proved most unforthcoming!

In Britain the craze was almost as strong, and it had many enthusiastic supporters, including Sir Arthur Conan Doyle (yes, him again). Slowly but surely over the course of the century, however, the number of fakes, frauds and cheats exposed by investigators helped ensure that few people took it seriously. The introduction of the Fraudulent Mediums Act in 1951 also helped. These days mediums are far less showy in the main, relying on techniques similar to those used by magicians who claim to be able to mind-read to persuade their audience that they have paranormal powers. Nowadays, most sensible people regard the topic as being about as scientific or likely to be true as a horoscope or a palm-reading.

Voices of the Dead

Among the most bizarre 'evidence' for the existence of an afterlife as a bodiless spirit is the 'Electronic Voice Phenomenon' (EVP), discovered in 1959 by Swedish musician and film producer Friedrich Jürgenson. Playing back a location recording of birdsong, he was startled to hear a faint male voice talking in Norwegian – about birdsong. The tape had been a new one and he had not heard anyone speaking near him in the remote spot where he had made the recording. It was just the first of many messages he was to detect on tapes; soon, on another spool, he heard what he believed to be the voice of his dead mother.

His work was continued by Latvian-born psychologist Dr Konstantin Raudive. Before his death in 1974, he recorded more than 100,000 messages from 'beyond' (OK, more usually from the radio, tuned to a dead channel), which have become known as Raudive Voices. However, an assessment of a typical case by a British researcher, David Ellis, revealed that Raudive may not have been picking up voices of the dead after all.

Here's a typical set of messages from 'the dead' according to Raudive: 'Glaube du Cedin ... Romani

Niowald zamuchils … ich folgu you tonight.' ('Believe you, Cedin – Romani Niowald is deathly tired – I follow you tonight.') Other people, on hearing the sensational tape, picked out something else through the fuzz: the voice of then-Radio Luxembourg DJ David 'Kid' Jensen, delivering a trailer for a show that ended 'It's all for you, tonight, at one o'clock.' Raudive had done nothing more than tape it off the radio, amidst a wash of interference.

At the time of his death, Raudive, undeterred by such revelations, had embarked on a new study, an analysis of the chirps made by a budgie called Putzi which, Raudive believed, was relaying messages from its dead owner. Cheep! Sigh.

Rattling Ghosts

The different divisions into which we have divided ghosts do, of course, have very blurred edges. It is sometimes little more than a matter of opinion as to whether a phantom is a Recording or a Haunting Ghost, say. The line between Hauntings and poltergeists is especially hazy, because many ghostly encounters show signs of both types of phenomena. This causes some problems, since investigators are now becoming convinced that the poltergeist is not a ghost at all – which has implications for the other types, too.

The word is German, from *poltern*, 'to make a loud noise' and *Geist* for 'ghost': noisy ghost. Oddly, the German for poltergeist is *Spuk*. As with all ghosts, there are plenty of misconceptions about poltergeists, many of them deriving from scary horror films such as the *Poltergeist* series.

The reality is quite different. Your average poltergeist may well be mischievous but it will never deliberately try to harm a human being; although objects may fly about, they always seem to be aimed away from anybody who gets too near. On the other hand, they do love smashing things, which perversely is good news for a ghost

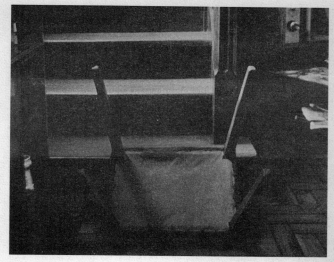

Chair tossed downstairs by a poltergeist, Ipiranga, Brazil, 1973.

investigator for one simple reason: evidence! Also encouraging, in a sense, is the fact that alleged poltergeist cases are now the most common form of haunting, and they are on the increase.

The activities of an alleged poltergeist can range (even in the same case) from unnerving noises to items of furniture being flung about wildly. In the gentlest cases, there may be little more than a bit of rapping or knocking, or doorbells and telephones ringing without an identifiable cause. Curtains may billow and doors slam without there being a draught. A stronger infestation may include objects that seem to move of their own accord, whether pushed, slid off shelves or even flung – though in most cases it's only the end result that people notice, and the route it took has to be worked out from where the now-broken object ends up! Electrical objects may play up or operate without being started. There may be cold spots and unusual smells. Note that this all sounds as if things are happening continually, but it is more usual for incidents to be infrequent and they may be spaced out over weeks or months. However, in the rarest cases, featuring a very angry spirit indeed, there may be utter pandemonium. Glass and mirrors may shatter, doors could open and close, water may form in pools, ghostly music or the cries of a baby may be heard, phones may ring incessantly, machines may start without power, light-bulbs could short and explode, and so on.

However, in all this the poltergeist will never actually make a physical appearance. As a result, all the strange things that happen will appear to be doing so as if by magic. It is for this reason that many people regard poltergeists as angry spirits rather than true ghosts – perhaps suggesting that there is not a dead person behind it at all – or alternatively they will look for scientific explanations within the human mind.

In an apparently genuine poltergeist infestation, each of these events will have to be proved as having no readily explainable cause. It's too easy to attribute a bit of forgetfulness or prank-playing to a poltergeist, and for each apparently genuine case there are many hundreds of fakes or mistakes. Much of the activity associated with such an infestation will appear to be going against the laws of nature – there is a big difference between a few pebbles thrown from behind a wall and the hands of a clock whizzing round at high speed!

Past polts

Some of the ghostly encounters recorded in olden times could, in fact, have been attributable to poltergeists. In the year 858 in Bingen-am-Rhein, Germany, for example, there is report of some nuisance caused by 'devils': 'Stones were thrown about by a malignant spirit, or so it was thought, and they struck the walls of simple dwellings as if with a hammer.' Since the affair also managed to draw attention to the dodgy activities of a farmer, it could even have been an early case of a poltergeist being faked to draw attention to something more serious! Whatever the truth, it seems correct to say that poltergeist activity has been recorded throughout the world, over many centuries, though it is only in the last century that we have put a specific name to the phenomenon.

Many more cases have been recorded over the years, in a wide range of cultures, from Kampala to Croatia. In 1661, Joseph Glanvill, the early ghost investigator, recorded the tale of the Phantom Drummer of Tedworth. A magistrate in the town, a Mr Mompesson, had sent a man to jail for annoying local people and begging with a fake licence. The magistrate also confiscated his drum and kept it in his house – only to find that something unseen was banging on it all day and night! The beggar, William Drury, told a visitor in prison that he was worried that he was somehow causing the drumming from a distance. In the end, Drury was transported to Australia, having been convicted of stealing a pig, and the drumming stopped.

Such a case was confined to a very specific item and place. A famous modern file deals with a far more widespread phenomenon. For several months at the end of 1981 and on into the following year, the residents of five houses in Thornton Road, Birmingham, complained of stones being thrown at their windows during the night. The police investigated. They could not get any fingerprints from the stones, so they started a surveillance using infra-red cameras and image-intensifiers. The stone-throwing continued as much as ever, but nothing else moved at night save for the local cats and foxes. After 300 man-hours, and still without an answer – and having solved five murders in the meantime – Birmingham CID gave up and went home, leaving the case open. Typically, the report stops there – for all we know stones are still flying in Thornton Road.

That case took place exclusively outdoors, but the best-known form for a poltergeist to take is as a range of indoor incidents, as we described earlier. However, not every poltergeist is an entirely unwelcome visitor. The Newman family of Sheffield awoke in the middle of the night in January 1982 to a depressingly familiar sound. The poltergeist which had been plaguing their flat for more than a year, throwing ornaments and household objects around and making loud banging noises, was at it yet again. This time, however, the father of the household, Derek Newman, lost his temper. He grabbed something heavy and flung open the bedroom door – to find the hallway full of smoke, because the flat was on fire! The family escaped in time and afterwards were very grateful to their friendly neighbourhood poltergeist.

Casebook: The Rosenheim poltergeist

We'll get on to the theories about poltergeists in a moment, but first we should look more closely at the landmark case which allowed scientists to study a ferocious infestation as it happened. As a result of their observations we are able to make more educated guesses about the phenomenon.

In the winter of 1967, a lawyer's office in Rosenheim in southern Germany began to be plagued by peculiar incidents. At first they were infrequent, but as the days passed they became more common. Initially, the telephones began to play up. They would all ring at the same time though nobody was on the other end, or the line would be disrupted by irritating clicking noises. Phone engineers couldn't pin-point the problem and were convinced the devices were working fine. After some weeks they gave up and passed the problem over to the Post Office. Their experts installed a meter to monitor every call. It revealed that dozens of calls were being registered from telephones that staff swore on oath had not been used. On one particular day, the Speaking Clock had been rung forty-six times in fifteen minutes, which was impossible for a human to manage in the days before number-memory phones. It was also pointed out that all the staff wore watches and could hear the chimes of at least two nearby church clocks.

As nerves began to fray, other office equipment started to misbehave. Fluorescent light-strips repeatedly twisted themselves out of their sockets, bulbs exploded, drawers shot out of desks and developing fluid gushed from a photocopier. More experts were called in, including electricians and a team of eminent physicists. They spent a day jumping up and down to try to re-create the motion of violently swinging lamps, but nothing seemed to simulate it. The power was cut off and the office's machines run from a generator, but the phenomenon continued. Finally, Germany's foremost parapsychologist, Dr Hans Bender, arrived with his team, and to him the conclusion was obvious: poltergeist.

He discovered several key clues. Odd things happened only during office hours. With the electricity cut off, power surges couldn't be to blame. It wasn't all a prank, since incidents had been caught on video-tape as they actually happened. Suspicion fell on a nineteen-year-old clerk called Annemarie Schneider. She was given a few days off; when she was absent from the office there was peace, but, when she returned, so did the chaos. She twitched oddly when anything was happening. One day a researcher noticed a lamp start to swing wildly when Annemarie walked under it. They began to keep a close watch on her, suspecting her of somehow doing it all physically. But when an immense oak cabinet hopped more than thirty centimetres despite weighing nearly two hundred kilos, they decided that she was generating the poltergeist phenomenon, but not deliberately. Further investigation revealed that she was from a country background and did not like working in the city so far away from her family, and this made her tense and unhappy

She was finally dismissed from the office staff in January 1968 and peace returned at last. Annemarie was studied by Dr Bender at the Freiburg Institute, but she could produce no special phenomena; it seemed that only extreme stress could cause it to happen. However, away from the scientists she could not hold down a steady job as the phenomena kept returning, and it only faded when she gave it all up and got married.

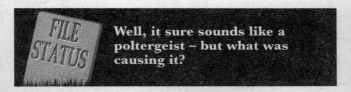

FILE STATUS

Well, it sure sounds like a poltergeist – but what was causing it?

It's a mind thing

Once again, the first possible explanation for the polter-geist phenomenon has to be that it is a fake. There are cer-tainly plenty of cases of frauds in the files. In the 1980s a case was brought to an American court by the family of an old woman, Catherine Noodyke, who, they claimed, had been driven mad by crazy voices and mysteriously moving objects. Her young husband had pretended there was a poltergeist, the claim went on, so that he could divorce her after five years, having fleeced her of over two million dollars.

Back in 1902, the respected psychic researcher, Frank Podmore, said, 'We have no good evidence for anything having been done which could not have been done by a girl or boy of slightly more than average cunning and naughtiness.' Dr Bender of Rosenheim fame would agree with that. He once videotaped a little girl, supposedly the focus of a poltergeist, and revealed that all she really wanted was more attention. When her parents tucked her up in bed and left her alone, she would run across the room, return with an ornament, then throw it on the floor with a crash. She would hop back into bed and call out for her mother.

More seriously, there have been several fraudulent poltergeist claims invented by people who wanted to get rehoused by their local council; however, many local authorities cottoned on to that swindle pretty quickly.

If the phenomena are not being faked, though – and in some cases expert researchers have certainly managed to rule out any trickery – what causes them? Scientists, always anxious to avoid using the word 'paranormal', suggest the problem may be power surges. In mid-December 1983, in Honey Tye, Suffolk, villagers fled from their homes as light-bulbs exploded and various electrical appliances switched themselves on and burnt out. The Eastern Electricity Board said that it was just a mystery surge in power that their safeguards, for once, had failed to prevent.

Even rarer are various types of electro-magnetic fields. It is thought that these can be generated by nearby radar installations, radio masts or microwave transmitters, or even electricity pylons. Researchers have suggested that when waves of different wavelengths meet, they may interfere with one another and build up, almost like an electro-magnetic tornado, to create a 'hot spot'. People caught within such build-ups may develop allergies, have blackouts, hear voices and see strange visions. Appliances may malfunction or burn out – or stay on and refuse to be switched off. However, we are far into the realms of the theoretical now, and much more research needs to be done before we can understand these very rare cases. Other theories have pointed the finger at subtle earth tremors, buried gas-pipes, subterranean rivers and tidal patterns. None of them has, as yet, come to much – but the scientists are still testing them thoroughly.

In the absence of any fully worked-out scientific solution, there is some support for a paranormal explanation. There are three basic strands, believers have proposed. First, the poltergeist could really be a spirit, a supernatural being that lives in another dimension, from where it causes trouble. The second is that the phenomena are totally powered from inside a living person using a wild form of telepathy, triggered by extreme stress or trauma. The third combines the two: the ghost (or, less controversially, some unknown natural energy) is the cause, but it needs a stressful person's powers to open the door and let it loose.

Of those, the most credible (comparatively) is number two. It is said to work like a mental version of a scream of frustration or anger. Imagine a person who gets so angry that he or she screams at the top of their voice, and the shout is so loud or high-pitched that a window or a drinking glass breaks. Replace that audible scream with a mental one, transmitted by some form of telepathic power. Sure, it still sounds as if it's founded deep in the realms of fantasy, but there are some persuasive details. It is clear from most poltergeist cases that the phenomenon is based round a single member of a household. Of course this points to a naughty child playing practical jokes, but not in every case. In fact, the most likely person to be associated with such events is an adolescent teenage girl, one who is either a little backward or exceptionally intelligent, who is ill or nervous, frustrated or angry. She cannot control her 'power' to cause the mayhem we associate with a poltergeist, the theory continues, and eventually it fades as she grows up.

Well, it's all very far-fetched and has no conclusive proof to back it up. It also requires proof of the existence of the forces that might power it, such as ESP or telekinesis – which are a long way from being added to the likes of the laws of gravity. The experts are still working on it – but, if it was true, it would certainly explain why your elder sister is so grumpy all the time!

The Real Ghost Investigators

The *X-Files* has done a lot for the image of professional ghost investigators. Unfortunately, there isn't an FBI or MI6 department that looks into such matters, at least officially, and most investigators are more likely to be jolly types in sensible jumpers and/or beards than a pair of glamorous Americans in expensive raincoats. In fact, when people think they have seen a ghost they don't do anything much, just mark it down to either a hallucination or a genuine but perfectly acceptable encounter. If something more drastic is going on, such as an alleged poltergeist throwing stones, the police will be called in. Ninety-nine times out of a hundred they will solve the case and bring the all-too-real perpetrators to book. However, once in a blue moon there will be a phenomenon which defies easy explanation, and that's when the real ghost investigators are called in.

The SPR, the ASSAP and the Ghost Club

The Society for Psychical Research grew out of Cambridge University's Ghost Society in the middle of the last century. Its first president, Henry Sidgwick, was a famous paranormal expert and the principles he laid down still apply to its thousand or so members today. As well as ghosts, the SPR also investigates cases of ESP, clairvoyance, hypnotism and other vague areas of pseudo-science. In its time it has uncovered more than its fair share of fakes – and just a few cases that continue to defy rational explanation. The SPR's headquarters – coincidentally located above a funeral director's premises in London! – are home to their incredible library, which is crammed with works, from major reference books to private journals and even 'ghostly writings'. It holds regular meetings and conferences, and many local ghost societies are affiliated with it.

The Association for the Scientific Study of Anomalous Phenomena (ASSAP) is a smaller and newer organization, based in Frome in Somerset, that pursues a similar line to the SPR. Many of the most famous ghost investigators will belong to both organizations. The Ghost Club, meanwhile, was founded back in 1862 by a bunch of enthusiastic amateurs, and its members still share some of that original gung-ho zeal for spooks. Currently led by Commander Bill Bellars, it primarily sponsors talks and lectures about famous hauntings, but it also organizes Ghostwatches.

Most countries will have some form of serious ghost-investigating society. Across the Atlantic, for example, the SPR has a sister organization in the American Society for Psychic Research, based in Boston. Other important groups include the New York-based American Parapsychology Foundation. Similar groups are found in the capital cities of most Westernized countries – for wherever you find ghosts you'll find ghost investigators.

Local groups

That accounts for the number of local ghost clubs round Britain, one of the world's most haunted and historical countries. There's probably a club near you. A typical group will hold regular meetings and talks where serious cases are discussed and more legendary stories are told. They may organize ghost walks or even all-night vigils in nearby haunted houses. Now and then, a ghostly encounter will make it into the local newspaper and you'll see the group's investigators snooping around, trying to get to the bottom of things. Usually, however, they won't all be like the Ghostbusters UK from Grimsby, who whizz about in their Ecto 1-like 'Ghostmobile' crammed with high-tech gear, just as in the famous movies.

Ghostwatching

If you want to have a real – albeit slim – chance of spotting a ghost, probably the best way to do so is to sign up for an organized event. This will also ensure that your investigations are safe and well supervised, which is obviously a good thing, and often a lot of fun.

The most basic form of organized event will be a ghost walk or trail. This may be a guided tour through a historic local building, with an expert from the town's ghost club telling all the gory details of the different phantoms legend says lurk thereabouts. These will give you a good grounding in the ghosts of your area and may suggest cases for further study. Obviously, such events are intended for the general public and tourists, so the stories you are told may be exaggerated and unproven. Worse, we have heard of some ghost walks where actors dress up as spooks and leap out on people. However, the ghosts seem to be getting their own back – on one ghost walk on the Isle of Wight in 1993, Mary Johnson and Robert LeBrecht were hiding in the shadows ready to leap out when ghostly footsteps crunched across the gravel and scared their socks off! Good thing too.

If you are looking for something more serious, track down a Ghostwatch. This where a group of people, perhaps sponsored for charity, will spend a night out at a haunted castle or mansion. Wrapped up in a sleeping-bag with some hot cocoa and listening to people telling ghost stories can be great fun. It will also show you at first hand how people contrive to scare themselves when nothing very spooky is going on – on a Ghostwatch every owl-hoot and bat-squeak will sound like the approach of a headless phantom!

The various ghost organizations also organize Ghostwatches, but these are not done for entertainment but to study real cases of possible hauntings. On one of these, the investigators will have to take it all far more seriously and monitor their equipment all night. However, to get on one of these, you will need to be a society member with a good track-record in ghost investigating.

If you see a ghost

As this book has, sadly perhaps, made clear, very few people, if any at all, really see actual ghosts. As an investigator, you will find it twice as hard – for some reason, it seems, ghosts seem to be able to detect experts and sneak out of the back door while you are coming in at the front with your gear. If, wonder of wonders, you do witness an incident that you think might be genuine, here's what you should do.

Get a record: First, try to get what you are seeing down on film, as many shots as you can. Try, amidst all the panic, to stay calm and get clear shots, in focus and with that darn lens cap off. If you can, frame the object against recognizable landmarks, such as a tree or people, so it will be possible to work out how big it might have been. If you don't have a camera to hand, draw a sketch as soon as possible after the sighting; if it moved, draw several. You don't need to be Leonardo da Vinci, but include as many details as you can recall. Similarly, if it's a ghostly noise you are hearing, get that tape rolling! (We're not sure what you should do if there's a nasty niff – probably just all point at one another and hold your nose.)

Write down everything that happened as soon as you can – and definitely before you discuss the case with other people. Try to include the size, shape, colour, whether it

A ghostly monk manifests during the Coventry Freeman's Guild dinner, 1985 – yet nobody saw a thing . . .

was transparent or solid, walked or floated, every last detail. Include senses other than your sight, such as any strange sensations, like a temperature drop. Also describe the weather conditions, the time and if any other people were present. Make sure you have a record of the exact location.

Get other witnesses: If more than one person sees an apparition, you have a far better chance of being taken seriously. Get them to take photos, make drawings and write down their own account too. A record of their names and addresses will also help. Try to assess how reliable they are and whether they believe unquestioningly in the existence of ghosts of every type, that sort of thing.

When dealing with witnesses, keep their accounts separate. Try not to discuss details of what happened with them until they have written down their own version. It's all too easy for someone to say, for example, 'No, the ghostly monk was taller than that, and grey rather than black.' Before you know it, you'll be changing your story because you've started to doubt it, and the Truth will have slipped away.

Tell people: This part may prove the trickiest, or at least somewhat embarrassing. If you are pretty certain that what you saw was definitely a ghost, you have some evidence, and you're prepared to stand by your story (and perhaps even risk being branded a bit of a weirdo), contact the authorities. In most cases this will be the local ghost group or the SPR. There are contact addresses at the back of this book. They will want as much detail as you can give them. They may have heard from other witnesses, and again may already have a logical explanation for you.

Important: If you are genuinely concerned or frightened by anything that you think has happened, tell an adult immediately. There will usually be a simple explanation, but sometimes we can't help but scare ourselves irrationally. Ghost investigating should be fun; if you are worried in any way, talk to your parents at once.

One final word, just to repeat what we said earlier: don't make hoax reports or fake photos. Hoaxers always get found out, sooner or later, and boy, do they look stupid when it happens.

This Haunted Isle

Ghosts are said to haunt just about everywhere. As we have seen, if the stories are to be believed, they can infest buses and banks, theatres and tower blocks. The most famous ghostly sites, however, still seem to belong in the 'haunted old mansion' category – allegedly, at least. The following few pages list some of the most widely known haunted sites. There are many, many more round the country and abroad. If we have missed out your favourite, please forgive us for the omission; we crammed in as many as we could!

If you want to go on a Ghostwatch, these places may prove to be just the ticket. Many will hold organized ghost walks or even all-night vigils. Of course there is no guarantee that a genuine ghost will actually turn up and try to spook you, but the experience could prove fun. When visiting these places, ensure that you go only to areas where you have permission. We have tried to list only those places where the public are allowed in, but they may be closed at certain times or have changed hands. Anyway, these should get you started …

ENGLAND

Avon
Almondsbury: The Bowl pub is haunted by the ghost of a French girl, Elizabeth Maronne, and the ruins of the Tudor Over Court are home to a white lady.

Bath: A schoolboy on one of the many ghost tours in 1976 saw a tall phantom with white hair; later seen by others. The Grey Lady in the Theatre Royal is always heralded by the scent of jasmine, while the Man in the Black Hat haunts the Assembly Rooms.

Bristol Cathedral: Home to a ghostly monk in a grey habit.

Brockley: A little woman in brown hurries about the church; in Brockley Wood there is a ghostly coach, an old woman and a clergyman.

Hanham Abbots: A ghostly nun haunts the road outside Hanham Court.

Bedfordshire

Aspley Guise: A ghost highwayman, obviously identified as Dick Turpin, still rides through the village.

Kensworth: The path to the local church is haunted by a headless milkmaid.

Woburn: Historic Woburn Abbey is full of ghosts: a man in a top hat, an unhappy woman in the summerhouse, and a monk in a brown habit.

Berkshire

Bisham: The abbey is haunted by Lady Elizabeth Hoby who murdered her son in 1609 because he couldn't write without making a mess.

Cookham Dean: A vicar's wife saw a vague shadow and felt a massive temperature drop in the church in 1979.

Easthampstead: The Iron Age hill-fort at Caesar's Camp is home to phantom sounds of battle.

Kintbury: Ghost in a wide-brimmed hat and a black cloak.

Windsor Castle: Home to many ghostly royals, including Henry VIII, Elizabeth I, Charles I, George III; also a great many ordinary ghosts around too. Further ghosts seen in Windsor Great Park.

Buckinghamshire

Ellesborough: A man in medieval clothes has appeared to people in the local church.

High Wycombe: Hughenden Manor was the home of the Victorian prime minister, Benjamin Disraeli; his ghost has been seen by many visitors.

Middle Claydon: Florence Nightingale once lived at Claydon Hall; a grey lady may or may not be her.

Cambridgeshire

Holywell: Every 17th March, Ye Olde Ferryboat Inn is witness to the ghost of poor Juliet Tewsley, who drowned herself after an unhappy love affair

Huntingdon: Nun's Bridge is haunted by a nun, of course, but she is accompanied by a ghostly nurse.

Kimbolton: Catherine of Aragon died here, and she still pops back now and then.

Wandlebury: The ancient hill-fort has been the site of many apparitions, especially black dogs.

Wicken Fen: This spooky expanse of marshland is home to the occasional will-o'-the-wisp, and has been home to a black dog.

Cheshire

Farndon: The bridge across the Dee is haunted by two ghostly children, whose cries are heard on stormy nights.

Gawsworth: The church is haunted by Mary Fitton, one of Elizabeth I's ladies-in-waiting.

Monk's Heath: A spooky grey lady stalks Capesthorne

Hall, and other sinister figures have been seen in the grounds.

Stoak: A headless duck (!) used to haunt a lane from Stoak to Stanney. Quack!

Cornwall
Hudder Down: A sinister man in black, Deadman's Cove.

Penhale: Legend says there's a town buried under the sand-dunes; its bells ring on stormy nights.

Cumbria
Levens: The Elizabethan Levens Hall is haunted by a pink lady and a grey lady.

Derbyshire
Edale: Many have heard the sounds of ghostly horses galloping near the church.

Shatton: A ghostly old man dressed in a farmer's smock and carrying a lantern has been seen in this village on several occasions.

Devon
Berry Pomeroy Castle: Ghosts, including sounds of a crying baby and a woman in a long hooded cape.

Exeter Cathedral: Phantom nun appears near south wall of the nave, usually at 7 p.m.

Lustleigh: In 1956, two women riding over Hunter's Tor encountered a large medieval hunting party, complete with greyhounds.

Lydford Castle: Judge Jeffreys haunts here, sometimes in the form of a black pig.

Postbridge: On nearby Cater Common, a black dog has been seen several times since the war. In the 1920s, several drivers were involved in accidents caused by large invisible hands pulling their steering wheels to one side.

Stoke: The vicar of the local church saw a hooded monk in 1973; other sightings followed.

Uplyme: The Black Dog Inn commemorates several sightings.

Wistman's Wood, Dartmoor: Legendary home of the Wish Hounds, huge ghostly black dogs. Woof!

Dorset

Bottlebush Down: Ghost horseman seen on the Roman Road, 1924.

Corfe Castle: Several ghosts, including a headless woman, seen in the last two decades.

Isle of Portland: The Tow Dog has been seen all over the island.

Sandford Orcas: Ancient manor house with more than its fair share of ghosts – fourteen in all! A lady in green; a lady in red who turns up at 11.50 p.m. on many evenings; a monk; an Elizabethan lady; and previous owner Sir Hubert Medlycott; also a ghost dog and the sound of a ghostly spinning wheel and a harpsichord.

Shaftesbury Abbey: Ghostly monk, who appears to be walking on his knees.

Wool: A phantom coach roams the lanes near Hethfelton House.

Don't go looking for Borley Rectory; it's now two bungalows.

Essex

Borley: The infamous location of Borley Rectory, now flattened and built over, was opposite the church.

Canewdon: The churchyard houses a woman in a wide, old-fashioned dress and bonnet.

Hadstock: The old Saxon church is haunted by a 'pleasant old gentleman'.

St Osyth: The priory grounds are home to a mysterious figure in white.

Waltham Abbey: A ghostly monk stalks the graveyard of Abbey Church.

Gloucestershire

Bisley: A group of headless men have been seen at the barrow at Money Tump.

Deerhurst: A ghostly Victorian woman has been seen around St Mary's Church.

Kempsford: Watch out for a silent monk, a boy in lace breeches, a knight and a frightened mother.

Littledean: Dean Hall is home to many ghosts, including duelling brothers and an ill-treated black manservant.

Prestbury: Once the site of a medieval bishop's palace; haunted by a dark abbot, two horsemen, a woman playing a spinet – and a man on a bike (more recent one, that).

Winchcombe: Sudeley Castle is haunted, surprisingly not by Catherine Parr (who is buried here), but by Janet, a Victorian housekeeper.

Hampshire

Basing: Oliver Cromwell is said to walk near the ruins of Basing House.

Beaulieu: Many reports of monks seen and heard chanting at the abbey, and incense smelt.

Breamore House: A lady in a bonnet who appears in order to indicate when the current owner will die.

Hayling Island: Churches at South Hayling now under the sea; ghostly ringing still heard.

Winchester: Ghost in old-fashioned clothing seen by a prisoner in the Castle Hall in 1973.

Hereford & Worcester

Goodrich: The ruined castle here sometimes rings to the plaintive cries of two drowned lovers.

Kington: Sir Thomas 'Black' Vaughan of Hergest Court, a wicked man of the fifteenth century who 'came back stronger and stronger all the while', still roams here; a black dog is thought to be his.

Hertfordshire

Knebworth House: The Radiant Boy, the death-warning naked child of the Lytton family, sometimes appears; the sound of 'Jenny Spinner' weaving is occasionally heard, and a phantom nobleman walks the picture gallery.

Markyate Cell: The ghost of Lady Catherine Ferrers, the basis for 'The Wicked Lady' in the classic film.

Minsden: Someone seemingly captured the eerie chapel's ghostly monk on film in 1908.

St Albans: The abbey is haunted by ghostly monks, who have been heard chanting.

Humberside

Burton Agnes: The hall here is home to the ghostly skull, 'Owd Nance'.

Leven: The road at White Cross was haunted by a ghostly woman who would scare riders.

Isle of Man

Douglas: Harold Tower is haunted by the spectre of a young servant girl.

Langness: The graveyard of the ruined church on St Michael's Island is full of those who died at sea; some poor sailors cannot rest, it is said.

Peel: The castle was once visited by the Moddey Dhoo, a fearsome phantom Black Dog.

Isle of Wight

Farringford Hall: Once the home of poet Alfred, Lord Tennyson, he is still seen in the grounds.

Quarr Abbey: Old ruins in the grounds are said to be haunted by Eleanor of Aquitaine – who has no connection with the area!

Kent

Canterbury Cathedral: Several ghostly monks and Roman soldiers but, oddly, no Thomas à Becket.

Dover Castle: A headless drummer boy from Napoleonic times haunts the castle; in the nearby Roman lighthouse, the Pharos, people have seen a Roman soldier and a monk.

Kemsing: At the end of December a ghostly knight is said to kneel in prayer in Kemsing Church.

Pluckley: Many ghosts seen here, including a white dog and a woman in white.

Rochester: At the castle, Lady Blanche de Warenne haunts the battlements and ghostly footsteps have been heard. Meanwhile, Charles Dickens, once a resident, is said to stroll round the Corn Exchange.

Lancashire

Wycoller: Once a year a ghost horseman gallops through the grounds of the restored Wycoller Hall.

Leicestershire

Leicester: Several historic buildings are haunted, including St Margaret's Church, Friar Lane and the former Holy Cross Priory.

Newtown Linford: Lady Jane Grey's spectral black coach sometimes rides round the grounds of the now-ruined Bradgate House.

Thringstone: A ghostly woman has been seen on the A512 near Grace Dieu Priory; she may be a nun.

Lincolnshire

Gunby: A pair of ghosts, murdered lovers, haunt the Ghost Walk at Gunby Hall.

Laughton: Builders have heard ghostly footsteps in the church tower.

London

Drury Lane: The Theatre Royal has a couple of the most famous ghosts in theatreland: a man in a riding coat and three-cornered hat, and music-hall star Dan Leno.

Greenwich: Charlton House, now a library, is haunted by a young servant girl carrying a dead baby in her arms.

Highgate Cemetery: Despite the legends, there are no vampires here, but it's still a very spooky place!

Tower of London: One of Britain's most haunted places, with a great many historical ghosts strolling the battlements, including Anne Boleyn 'wiv 'er 'ead tucked underneaff 'er arm'.

Westminster Abbey: A khaki-clad warrior has been seen near the Tomb of the Unknown Soldier; several monks have also appeared to people.

Middlesex

Enfield: Many people have seen the phantom coach, a huge black carriage drawn by four ghostly horses.

Norfolk

Blickling: Anne Boleyn is a very busy ghost; she also pops up at her birthplace, Blickling Hall. Her father also turns up sometimes, racing around in his coach.

Cromer: The cliff paths are home to Black Shuck.

Geldeston: The road to Bungay is often haunted by a ghostly coach lashed on by a headless horseman. Yikes!

Hickling Broad: A phantom woman in a white dress who punts across the water in her skiff. Near by, the priory has a ghostly monk.

Northamptonshire

Boughton: The ruins of St John's Church are haunted at Christmas by 'Captain Slash', a Georgian gang-leader.

Fotheringay: The eerie music which sometimes haunts the fifteenth-century church is said to date back to the time of Agincourt.

Naseby: The battlefield has often resounded to the sounds of war.

Northumberland

Blanchland: The Lord Crewe Arms is home to the red-robed figure of a Stuart woman, Dorothy Forster.

Haltwhistle: Featherstone Castle is roamed by a ghostly search party.

Hazelrigg: St Cuthbert's Cave is said to be haunted by the ghost of a medieval cattle-rustler.

Lindisfarne: The ancient abbey is wandered by the ghost of St Cuthbert, several ghostly monks and also a spectral white hound.

Seaton Delaval: A mysterious woman in grey haunts the hall. Another one!

Nottinghamshire

Newstead Abbey: The spooky ancestral home of poet Lord Byron is haunted by his ancestor, Little Sir John Byron, Byron's dog, a sinister Black Friar and a spectral lady in white, possibly Sophia Hyett, who was infatuated with the poet and cannot rest without him.

Nottingham Castle: The ghost of Roger Mortimer, Earl of March, haunts a tunnel beneath Castle Rock.

Oxfordshire

Burford: The nunnery was once a priory and is haunted by a brown monk; there have also been ghostly bells and the sound of singing from the garden.

Shropshire

Ellesmere: Bells thrown in Cole Mere by Cromwell's soldiers are said to ring on windy nights under the full moon.

Somerset

Exmoor: Ghostly horses can be heard on Winsford Hill; also Black Dog legend.

Sedgemoor: Ghostly sounds since the 1685 battle.

Staffordshire
Tamworth: Several different robed women haunt historic Tamworth Castle.

Suffolk

'Black Dog marks' at Blytheborough Church.

Bungay/Blytheborough: Two sites of churches attacked by the Black Dog of Bungay; marks remain on the door of Blytheborough Church, while there's a great weathervane topped by the hound itself at Bungay.

Bury St Edmunds: The ruined abbey is infested with many ghosts, especially phantom monks.

Dunwich: One the most famous 'drowned villages', its drowned bells can sometimes still be heard; the ruined Greyfriars Priory is also haunted.

Walberswick: The ruined church and the common are both haunted by ghostly figures.

Surrey

Bletchingley: The ghost of a woman seen repeatedly in the church.

Brooklands: The famous early racing circuit is still haunted by the sounds of revving engines, and sometimes the goggle-wearing figure of Percy Lambert.

Farnham: Several witnesses have seen services from previous times taking place in the church.

Guildford: Loseley House is haunted by a woman with staring black eyes.

Reigate: Woman in a long white dress walking in the churchyard, and a ghostly choir heard outside.

Silent Pool, near Guildford: Legend of Emma, drowned when King John spied her bathing and waded in to grab her (but see page 81).

Sussex

Arundel Castle: Four ghosts: a man in a grey tunic; a 'blue man'; a kitchen boy; and a girl in white.

Battle Abbey: A lady in red, a lady in grey and a ghostly monk.

Bosham: Vikings stole a bell from the church by boat, but it sank; it still answers the others.

Brighton: Royal Pavilion has an underground passage said to be stalked by the Prince Regent, who built it.

Crowborough: At the end of the last century, Jarvis Brook Road was haunted by a ghostly ... bag of soot!

Ditchling: Black Dog Hill has been the scene of ... you guessed it.

Hailsham: Thirteenth-century Michelham Priory haunted by a grey lady.

Hastings Castle: A woman in brown, possibly a nun, seen digging; Thomas à Becket also reported strolling in the ruins.

Pevensey Castle: Ghost of Lady Pelham strolls along the walls at dusk.

Stoughton: Ghostly warriors haunt the round barrows in Kingley Vale.

Washington: Ghost of a white-bearded man haunts the spooky tree glades at Chanctonbury Ring and invisible hoof-beats have been heard.

Warwickshire

Chadwick End: A group of phantom nuns often walks the road outside the manor.

Edgehill: The Civil War battle has been replayed here, and ghostly soldiers have been seen in the nearby area.

Preston-on-Stour: A ghostly farmer sometimes crosses the road and disappears into the wall of Alscot Park.

Warwick: The wonderful castle is home to several ghosts. The ruined old house at Guy's Cliff has rung to the sound of ghostly bells.

West Midlands

Aston: Aston Hall is haunted by a young girl who was walled up in her room for not marrying the man her father had chosen! A spectral Victorian woman has been seen in Aston Park

Wiltshire

Avebury: The standing stones still sometimes play back the lights and sounds of Victorian fairs. The nearby manor house is home to a monk and a Cavalier.

Bradford-on-Avon: The tiny Saxon church of St Laurence has been witness to several visions of medieval people taking communion.

Highworth: A ghostly man in the church here.

Savernake Forest: A strange old man at the Savernake Arms public house.

West Kennet: The Long Barrow on Midsummer's Day is haunted by a priest and his ghostly white dog.

Yorkshire

Doncaster: Twelfth-century Conisborough Castle, the setting for Sir Walter Scott's *Ivanhoe*, is home to a White Lady and a ghostly monk.

East Riddlesden: Up at the hall, the Risworth cradle rocks itself 'every' New Year's Eve; also a grey lady.

Haworth: The ghost of Emily Brontë is said to wander the windswept moors near her home.

Leeds: The gatehouse of Kirkstall Abbey, now a museum, is haunted by a ghostly abbot.

Sheffield: Beauchief Abbey, now ruined, is haunted by a white lady and a monk, possibly others.

Whitby: The ruined abbey here is haunted by its Dark Ages founder, St Hilda; also a coach-and-horses and a ghostly man in white robes.

York: The Treasurer's House was scene of the infamous Roman soldiers; other sites near by have also reported them. Holy Trinity Church has a ghostly nun.

WALES

Clywd

Llangollen: The strange black-and-white house at Plas Newydd is haunted by a pair of little old ladies in Victorian costume.

Mold: The eerie Jacobean manion at Plas Teg is home to the sad phantom of a grieving young girl from Georgian times.

Plas Pren: The ruined hunting lodge is haunted by a 'tall, luminous skeleton'!

Trelawnyd: A force of spectral Roman soldiers has been seen by the prehistoric cairn at Gop-y-Goleuni.

Dyfed

Carew Castle: A woman in white, possibly from the eleventh century, stalks the battlements.

Gorslas: The lake here, Llyn Llech Owen, is said to be home to a drowned land.

Talley: The ruined abbey is home to a ghostly cloaked man, possibly a monk.

Gwent

Penhow: The ghost of a maid still scurries around Penhow Castle.

Risca: Ghostly organ music has often been heard at the top of the prehistoric earthworks.

Tintern Abbey: A ghostly monk still lurks in these impressive ruins.

Gwynedd

Anglesey: The ghosts of Roman soldiers and druids haunt the valley where treasure was found in 1943 at Llyn Cerrig Bach.

Bardsey Island: Twenty thousand monks are said to be buried here; a few are rather restless.

Mid Glamorgan

Ogmore Castle – now that's spooky!

Caerphilly: The castle is haunted by a green-robed lady with goggle eyes; she is sometimes accompanied by spectral soldiers.

Cilfynydd: The wooded slopes above the brook are haunted by a white-clad lady.

Ogmore: The ruined castle is sometimes witness to a ghostly lady in white robes.

Powys

Llangorse Lake (Llyn Syfaddan): Sounds of a drowned town heard from under the lake.

Welshpool: Powis Castle is haunted by a man in a waistcoat and gold-trimmed hat.

South Glamorgan

Cardiff: The castle is home to a tall man in a red cloak, possibly the second Marquess of Bute.

West Glamorgan

Margam: The abbey ruins are home to a ghostly monk, it is said.

Oxwich: Many people have seen a ghostly white horse that walks on its hind legs.

Oystermouth: The ruined castle is haunted by a crying lady in white.

SCOTLAND

Borders

Newcastleton: Hermitage Castle has long had a bloodthirsty reputation. Evil Lord Soulis haunts the place, along with a white lady.

Central

Buchanan Castle: The derelict nineteenth-century house is reputed to be haunted by unearthly screams and moans that continue to terrify unwary passersby.

Stirling Castle: A phantom woman in pink walks from the castle to the church; there is also a green lady.

Fife

St Andrews: The cathedral, though partly collapsed, is haunted by a frequently seen woman in a white dress and veil.

Grampian

Castle Grant: The home of the Grants is stalked by a ghostly piper who still proclaims the Clan's defeat at Culloden; also a Recording Ghost of a maid in the dining-room.

Muchalls: The castle is haunted by the ghost of a young lady in green.

Highlands

Culloden: The old battlefield is said to echo still to the sound of soldiers.

Dornoch: The last witch to be executed in Scotland, Janet Horne, haunts the Witches Stone that marks where she died in 1772.

Loch Alsh: The striking Eilean Donan Castle is haunted by the ghost of an eighteenth-century Spanish sailor – which at least is different.

The road near Sligachan – and are those headlights?

Nigg Bay: Another legendary drowned village whose bells can still sometimes be heard.

Sligachan, Isle of Skye: The road is haunted by a phantom driverless car, or sometimes just its headlights.

Lothian

Linlithgow: The ancient Scottish royal palace is haunted by the ghost of a woman dressed in a bluish gown. St Michael's Church was where King James IV saw a ghostly man in blue who foretold his death at Flodden.

Strathclyde

Barcaldine: The castle, ancestral home of the Campbells, is stalked by the ghost of the eighteenth-century laird, Duncan Campbell.

Iona: Once the scene of Viking raids, a ghostly longboat, phantom monks and many spectral soldiers have been seen here.

Lendalfoot: The ruined Carleton Castle, perched high on the ridge, has echoed to ghastly ghostly screams.

Mull: The road through gloomy Glen More is home to a headless horseman.

Oban: Dunstaffgne Castle is occasionally visited by a mysterious green lady; the ghost of Flora MacDonald is also reputed to walk here.

Tayside

Glamis Castle: The legendary home of the Macbeths; several ghosts, including that of the murdered (but possibly only fictional!) Duncan and a ghostly carriage.

Letham: Scene of a ghostly re-enactment of a Pictish battle in 1950 (see page 43).

Two Knocks for No?

As you have been reading this book, you may have noticed that we have a lot of, well, uncomplimentary things to say about the subject of ghosts and whether they exist. This is because, quite simply, no one knows if they exist or not and there is no proof one way or another. Add to that the fact that almost every supposed sighting is either mistaken identity or wishful thinking, and the odds against ghosts being proven to exist get slimmer.

As a ghost investigator, this may be irrelevant. Even if there aren't any actual spooks lurking out there in the dungeons and halls all round the country, it is fascinating to study how such a confusion of beliefs develops. In effect, as a ghost investigator one can't help but end up studying the people who believe in ghosts as much as the ghosts themselves. Whatever your particular interest, you can always just sit back and regard each case as a fascinating ghost story.

And then again … there is always that lingering doubt in the back of one's mind. There is always that tiny percentage of files which have no explanation, which hint that, despite all the mistakes and fakes, there has to be something in the belief in ghosts. For the future, what is needed is proof – solid, undeniable proof. That's why the world needs ghost investigators, good honest people like yourself who can go out there and track down the truth, who won't be fooled by obvious missightings or swayed by obvious legends. Don't fall into the trap of seeing ghosts because you are looking for them; make up your mind based on the facts alone. Let this book be your guide, and your most trusted piece of equipment be your powers of reason.

We have every faith in you. Good luck!

Field Support for Investigators

Ghost investigators out in the field should trust no one, examining everything in their search for the Truth. However, there are a few reliable independent organizations to which investigators can turn for assistance.

You should also do your research. Know your stuff: keep files on all the famous cases, swot up on the classic hoaxes and misidentifications, get involved. Here are some handy resources which may come in very useful in your continuing investigations.

Organizations

As you can imagine, many of the people who join ghost-investigating societies, particularly local ones, are believers. They want to believe that the strange blur they saw while falling asleep was indeed the Mad Monk of Maidstone, regardless of the facts. However, the larger groups have learnt how to be far more objective. They know that not every rustle or scrape is a ghost – because for years they're the ones who've sat out on Ghostwatches and not seen a thing! They will say when something definitely isn't a haunting, and they are prepared to admit that some incidents are unproven. If you think you have seen a ghost, contact the SPR or your local ghost group.

Society for Psychical Research (SPR): Investigates all paranormal activities, not just ghosts. About a thousand full-time members and many more affiliates. Organizes monthly lectures, also study days, weekend workshops and an annual conference; also sends out the quarterly *Journal of the SPR* and various irregular publications.

Address: 49 Marloes Road, Kensington, London W8 6LA

Association for the Scientific Study of Anomalous Phenomena (ASSAP): A more specialized, scientific-based group, with around 350 full members. Organizes Ghostwatches and regular meetings, and publishes the *ASSAP News* quarterly.

Address: Saint Aldhelm, 20 Paul Street, Frome, Somerset BA11 1DX

Local groups

Most large towns and cities have a local ghost group, especially if the location is renowned for having plenty of well-recorded spooks. They may organize ghost walks and even Ghostwatches. They may be populated by people who firmly believe that they've seen a ghost as well as by those interested in the scientific study of the subject; but at least they will be keen. To find your nearest group, ask in your local library or tourist information centre.

Further reading

A dedicated investigator will know his or her subject inside out. Unfortunately, it has to be said, far too many of the hundreds of ghost books that clog the shelves are written by believers, people who are looking, hoping, praying that there really is a life after death, rather than trying to explain what people are actually witnessing. Beware: everyone has an agenda!

Here are some of the most useful sources, both from rational writers and from some more biased believers, that you should be able to find in bookshops or order in your public library. Also look out for ghost guides to your area; many have been written by local authors, telling the stories of famous ghosts of a specific county or city. They tend to be less than sceptical about their subject, but they will point you to ghost legends local to your area.

A–Z of British Ghosts,
Peter Underwood

The Atlas of Magical Britain,
Janet and Colin Bord

The Case of the Cottingley Fairies,
Joe Cooper

Encyclopedia of Ghosts and Spirits,
Rosemary Guiley

Encyclopedia of the Unexplained,
Jenny Randles and Peter Hough

Encyclopedia of the World's Greatest Mysteries,
John and Anne Spencer

Fortean Times Weird Year 1996,
Joe McNally and James Wallis

The Ghost of Flight 401,
John Fuller

Ghostwatching,
John Spencer and Tony Wells

The Good Ghost Guide,
John Brooks

In Search of Ghosts,
Ian Wilson

Strange But True? Casebook,
Jenny Randles

The Unexplained,
Karl Shuker

The X-Files Book of the Unexplained vols. I & II,
Jane Goldman

The Unexplained CD-ROM

Fortean Times magazine

Psychic News magazine

Further watching

The show that started it all, *The X-Files*, is always great entertainment – but just because they show ghosts and other forms of the paranormal on the screen, that doesn't necessarily mean that they really have been proved to exist in real life. Keep your eyes open for many more TV programmes and blockbuster movies cashing in on the extraordinary success of *The X-Files*.

Many documentaries on the paranormal tend to be sensationalist or based on the unchallenged assertions of believers, but they are a great source of entertainment if nothing else. Look out for series like *Strange But True?*, *Fortean TV*, *The Unexplained*, *The Real X-Files*, *Equinox* and many, many more.

Films dealing with ghosts tend to fall into three basic types. There are gory horror movies in which the haunting is just an excuse to do in some dumb American college students; these are little more than blood-spattered updates of the grisly old Hammer horror movies about Dracula or Frankenstein and tell us nothing useful about ghosts. There are comedies, like *Ghostbusters* and *Casper*, where the ghosts are jolly, blobby things that slime people, and everyone lives happily ever after at the end; and there is romantic nonsense like *Ghost*. The best films about ghosts are the truly spooky ones, too often made in the days of black and white, in which genuinely strange things happen but no one runs around wielding a chainsaw. There is also a new film about the Cottingley fakes which was still on the 'coming soon' list at the time of writing; look out for it.

Further surfing

If you are lucky enough to have access to the Internet, you'll discover that it's a haven for a variety of paranormal enthusiasts. The Net's image as a free forum has made it an attractive place for spreading the craziest theories. As with all areas of your investigations, the Truth is hidden out there somewhere – but all too often amidst a huge swathe of barmy drivel.

World Wide Web:

EarthLight Productions Haunted Web Page: A pile of links to other haunted pages starts at http://www.primenet.com/~sgoodman/Halloween

Fortean Times: The popular magazine of the unusual on-line at http://www.forteantimes.com/

FutureNet: 'All the facts about the unexplained phenomena this world has to offer', it starts at http://www.geocities.com/SiliconValley/Park/5952/index.html

Ghost Stories: Scare yourself at http://www.midnet.sc.edu/ghost/ghosthp.htm

Haunted Corners of the World Wide Web: Scary stuff at http://www.nightmarefactory.com/corners.html

Haunted House of the Haunted: So this is haunted then? http://www.df.lth.se/~beaker/HHaut95/hhaut95.html

History of Borley Rectory: Posted by Marianne's son (!) at http://www.kdcol.com/~rvon/history.htm

Obiwan's UFO-Free Paranormal Page: No saucers at http://www.best.com/~dijon/ghosts/index.html

The Ooga Booga Page: Cool shivers and shakes from the haunted world.
http://star06.atklab.yorku.ca/~peterpan/index.html

The Shadowlands Ghosts page: More spooks at
http://users.aol.com/shadoland2/ghost.html

Strange Magazine: Including their updated Top Ten Strangest list, starts at
http://www.cais.net/strangemag/home.html

Spectre Search: A list of haunted places to visit in the USA from
http://www.airmail.net/~spectre1/source/page0.html

WWW Virtual Library: Archive X: A whole shelf devoted to the paranormal at
http://www.crown.net/X/

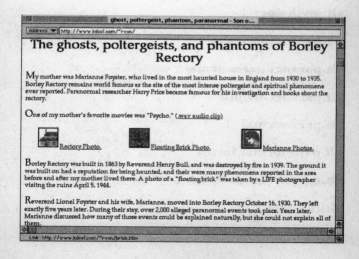

ghost, poltergeist, phantom, paranormal - Son o...

Address ▼ | http://www.kdool.com/~rvon/

The ghosts, poltergeists, and phantoms of Borley Rectory

My mother was Marianne Foyster, who lived in the most haunted house in England from 1930 to 1935. Borley Rectory remains world famous as the site of the most intense poltergeist and spiritual phenomena ever reported. Paranormal researcher Harry Price became famous for his investigation and books about the rectory.

One of my mother's favorite movies was "Psycho." (.wav audio clip)

Rectory Photo.   Floating Brick Photo.   Marianne Photos.

Borley Rectory was built in 1863 by Reverend Henry Bull, and was destroyed by fire in 1939. The ground it was built on had a reputation for being haunted, and their were many phenomena reported in the area before and after my mother lived there. A photo of a "floating brick" was taken by a LIFE photographer visitng the ruins April 5, 1944.

Reverend Lionel Foyster and his wife, Marianne, moved into Borley Rectory October 16, 1930. They left exactly five years later. During their stay, over 2,000 alleged paranormal events took place. Years later, Marianne discussed how many of those events could be explained naturally, but she could not explain all of them.

Link : http://www.kdool.com/~rvon/brick.htm

The X Chronicles: A Canadian magazine of the odd, weird and downright peculiar.
http://vaxxine.com/xchronicles

The X-Files: Fan website devoted to some TV show or other ...
http://www.rutgers.edu/x-files.html

Newsgroups:

alt.folklore

alt.folklore.computer

alt.folklore.ghost-stories

alt.folklore.urban

alt.life.afterlife

alt.misc.forteana

alt.mythology

alt.paranet.forteana

alt.paranet.paranormal

alt.paranet.skeptic

alt.paranormal

alt.paranormal.fortea

alt.sci.physics.new-the

alt.tv.x-files

uk.media.tv.sf.x-files

Spook Speak

Agent: Someone who appears to be the cause of a psychic phenomenon, such as a poltergeist, occurring.

Anniversary ghost: An apparition that is said to turn up every so often, such as every year.

Apparition: A supernatural form, such as a human- or animal-shaped ghost.

Apport: An object (such as a coin, jewellery, etc.) that appears 'out of nowhere' while a ghost or an apparition is around.

Asport: The opposite of apport – an object that disappears while, for example, a poltergeist is causing a nuisance.

ASSAP: The Association for the Scientific Study of Anomalous Phenomena.

Automatic writing: Making marks while apparently under the influence of a ghost.

Believer: A person who thinks that there definitely are ghosts and spirits haunting the planet.

Black dog: Large ghostly hound; many are said to haunt the wilder parts of Britain.

Cold spot: Unnaturally cool area of, say, a room.

Crisis apparition: An apparition that turns up to warn of a death or some other emergency.

Doppelgänger: A 'double', such as a ghostly duplicate of a person.

Ectoplasm: A fake substance allegedly made to appear by the energies of a ghost being transmitted through a medium; in reality, usually made of cotton wool.

ESP: Extra-sensory perception – transmitting or receiving knowledge using the mind alone.

Fortean: Relating to unusual phenomena, e.g. rains of fish; named after the pioneering investigator of such matters, Charles Fort.

Ghost: An apparition, thought to be an image of a dead being.

Ghostology: The study of ghosts.

Ghostwatch: An organized camp-out in the hope of witnessing a ghost.

Grey lady: A classic ghost: the hooded, grey-robed figure of a woman.

Hallucination: A vision of something not actually there, that may seem very real to the viewer.

Lemuria: Yearly ancient Roman festival to calm ghosts.

Living ghost: Like a crisis apparition, but the vision is of someone still alive.

Materialization: The sudden appearance of an object, as if out of thin air.

Medium: Someone who claims to be able to contact or sense ghosts.

OOBE: Out-of-Body Experience; a sense of leaving one's own body and floating up into the air.

Paranormal: Anything that cannot usually be explained by one of the five senses.

Phantom: Another word for a ghost.

Poltergeist: An unseen spirit that causes trouble by throwing objects around; may be caused by a human rather than a ghost.

Psychic: A human who is able to sense ghosts.

Psychokinesis (PK): Moving something using a mental or otherwise paranormal power; like telepathy.

Recording Ghost: An apparition that seems tied to one place and doesn't react to humans.

Seance: An organized gathering at which people try to contact ghosts.

Sensitive: Someone who is especially able to sense ghosts.

Shade: An old term for a ghost.

Spectre: Another word for a ghost.

Spirit: A bodiless being or a ghost.

Spook: Another word for a ghost; hence 'spooky'.

SPR: The Society for Psychical Research.

Telekinesis: The power to move something without touching it; see PK.

Time-slip: Temporarily visiting or witnessing, somehow, a period in history.

Trance: A semi-hypnotic state, hopefully making one more sensitive to ghosts.

Transmitter: A being that sends a vision of itself to someone else in another place or time.

Urban myth: A modern form of folk-tale, a story that people think is genuine but which is told all around the world as a 'true story'.

Vigil: A Ghostwatch.

INDEX

The UFO Investigator's Handbook

by Marc Gascoigne

The truth is in here . . .

UFOs, extra-terrestrials or just white lights and hoaxers – depending on who you believe, the world is either under constant threat from alien invasion or it is simply full of weirdos. But what is the truth? You can decide for yourself in this amazing new book.

* The early sightings – Foo fighters and airship scares
* Close encounters – the famous stories
* The Roswell incident – superbeing or plastic dummy?

Look at the facts, seek out the truth. Before you know it, you'll be investigating your very own *X-Files*™.